The Velvet Glove

The
Velvet Glove

NOEL B. GERSON

THOMAS NELSON INC., PUBLISHERS
Nashville • New York

Second printing

Library of Congress Cataloging in Publication Data

Gerson, Noel Bertram.
    The velvet glove.

    Bibliography: p.
    Includes index.
    1. Madison, Dolly Payne Todd, 1768–1849.   I. Title.
E342.1.G47   973.5′1′0924 [B]   75–23124
ISBN 0–8407–6472–3

"What an extraordinary, great lady she was! America will never know another like Mrs. Madison."

—ZACHARY TAYLOR
Twelfth President of the United States

The Velvet Glove

I

*O*n March 4, 1845, a few hours after his inauguration as eleventh President of the United States, James K. Polk walked the short distance from the White House to a modest dwelling on Lafayette Square in order to pay his respects to Mrs. Dorothea Payne Todd Madison, the widow of one of his greatest predecessors, and Americans of every political persuasion applauded. Later in the day, during the celebratory reception at the Executive Mansion, the new President rebuked a visitor who remarked that Dolly Madison was a Washington institution.

"Sir," he said, "I stand with my good friend and mentor, President Jackson, who called her a *national* institution."

Polk was too diplomatic to mention that, when he went to her home, he had come upon a shoeless Mrs. Madison running foot races with two teen-aged daughters of friends, impervious to the discomforts of the frozen ground. Perhaps the incident made no impression on him, because, like everyone who knew her, he accepted Mrs. Madison's belief that she needed the exercise. At the time she was in her seventy-seventh year.

Certainly Polk's visit could not have surprised her, and nothing could ruffle the old lady's composure. She had been close to every President since the founding of the nation. She had been the protégée of the austere George and Martha Washington, the friend of the reserved John and Abigail Adams. She had acted as the official hostess for the President during the eight-year administration of widower Thomas Jefferson, whom her husband had served as Secretary of State. She had then been First Lady in her own right for another eight years. Mrs. Madison had known the James Monroes intimately, had enjoyed a pleasant if cool relationship with John Quincy Adams, and had not only been close to Andrew Jackson, but had also been the first aristocrat to accept the blunt Old Hickory without reservation. Martin Van Buren had called on her frequently, William Henry Harrison had invited her to his inauguration, and she had been the first to approve of John Tyler's marriage to a young bride, whom she had promptly invited to the Madison estate in Orange County, Virginia.

Now the Polks had moved into the White House, the informal name she herself had given the Executive Mansion, and they were old friends, too. There were some people who exaggerated her power, but she had long asserted that she had none. "Politics," she had told her sister during James Madison's second administration, "is the business of men. I don't care what offices they may hold, or who supports them. I care only about *people*."

Because her concern for them was so obvious, people cared about Mrs. Madison in return. Every foreign dignitary who came to the United States, from the Marquis de Lafayette to Napoleon Bonaparte's relatives, paid a courtesy call on her, and soon discovered—frequently to his own surprise—that he was telling her his personal problems. During her husband's lifetime a steady stream of Senators and Supreme Court Justices, members of the House of Representatives, and Cabinet officers had traveled to the Madison plantation, Montpelier, where she had entertained them with a gracious hospitality that had been renowned. Now, when she was living in reduced circumstances in Washington, they came to see her for herself.

Men enjoyed her company because she put them at their ease, respected their confidence, and gave them advice they regarded as sage. Women were fascinated by her because she put on no airs, because even now in her midseventies she was the fashion leader whose innovative styles were copied throughout Europe as well as in the States. And her recipes were so famous that a hostess was certain her party would be a success if she announced that Mrs. Madison had told her how a dish should be prepared.

Above all, no one forgot that she was a heroine in her own right. During the nation's worst hour, when British troops had marched on Washington City during the War of 1812, she had risked her life to save some of the country's most valuable treasures. "Anyone would have done what I did," she said soon afterward, but her contemporaries saluted her courage, and so has posterity. She appreciated the praise, even though she thought it unwarranted, and her modesty was genuine. Married to a genius and surrounded by greatness, she took her own unusual attributes for granted, and laughed when she was told she was the greatest beauty of her era.

"If that be true," she told an admiring Lafayette when she was middle-aged, "it is my parents, not I, who deserve your felicitations. It was not I, sir, who determined the shape of my nose or the texture of my skin."

Her courage often expressed itself in unexpected ways. Living in an age when most Virginians accepted slavery, she expressed her detestation of the institution. She had loathed it long before she married James Madison and heard him denounce it. That attitude was typical of her. Despite the fact that she lived in a period when mem-

(11)

bers of her sex were expected to be nothing more than their husbands' appendages, she had a mind of her own and exercised it freely.

Her spirit of independence, perhaps, was the real secret of her popularity, and she had genuine stature in her own right. It is remarkable that so many women praised her and so few envied her.

President Zachary Taylor, the Mexican War hero whose exploits won him the White House, was not the most creatively imaginative of men. But he spoke for all of his fellow citizens when Dolly Madison died in 1849 at the age of eighty-one. "She will never be forgotten," he said, "because she was truly our First Lady for a half-century."

Dorothea, the first daughter of John Payne, Jr., and Mary Coles Payne, happened to be born on a farm in New Garden, North Carolina, now in Guilford County, on May 20, 1768. Her parents, aristocratic Virginians, were spending a year and a half on property they owned in North Carolina. This enabled Dolly to claim both states as her home, a term she also applied to Pennsylvania when she moved there later. She maintained this attitude for so many years that it is fairly safe to assume she was not being blandly political, but honestly thought of herself as a native of all three states.

Her family was comfortably situated, if not wealthy, and her ancestors on both sides were distinguished. William Coles, Dolly's maternal grandfather, was a blue-eyed, auburn-haired farmer who achieved success in Virginia after coming to the Colonies from Ireland. Dolly always said she inherited her eyes and hair from him, as well as her wit and her facile mind. His wife was a member of the aristocratic Winston family, known in Virginia for its beautiful women.

Some of Dolly's earliest memories were of her mother's

home, Coles Hill, in Hanover County. Nearby was a huge clapboard structure known as Scotchtown, which soon would become famous in its own right because one of her cousins would live there for a number of years. Patrick Henry, many years her senior, was already achieving renown in the House of Burgesses and emerging as a leader of the young intellectuals who were advocating the separation of the Colonies from Great Britain.

Dolly's paternal grandfather, the elder John Payne, was a gentleman of substance and a graduate of Oxford University, who had migrated to Virginia and established himself on a plantation in Goochland County. His wife, Anna Fleming, was a direct descendant of one of the early settlers in Jamestown, Sir Thomas Fleming.

The elder Payne, who served for many years in the Burgesses, was ever conscious of his responsibilities. For a long time he was a vestryman in the Episcopal Church, and he contributed substantial sums each year to the poor. When his nineteen-year-old son married Mary Coles he gave the newlyweds a tract of four hundred acres on Little Byrd Creek, and there the younger Payne built a home for his bride, a place that would know many additions as the family grew.

Grandfathers Payne and Coles were staunch supporters of the Church of England, but Dolly's parents were drawn to the Quaker faith, and in 1764 they became members of the Society of Friends. Mary Payne was active in the organization for the rest of her days. As Quakers, the Paynes were strongly opposed to slavery, but like so many other Southerners they owned a number of slaves, and their livelihood depended on the labor of the field hands on their expanding property. They and the contemporaries who shared their views did not think of themselves as hypocritical for continuing to enjoy the economic benefits of slavery while advocating its abolition. The best that can be said for them is that short of actually granting liberty to their slaves, they treated them like freedmen and paid them wages in addition to giving them food, shelter, clothing, and a measure of medical care. Dolly would inherit their attitudes.

There were already two sons in the family, six-year-old Walter and two-year-old William, when the first daughter came on the scene. Dolly was followed, in order, by Lucy, Anna, Mary, John, Isaac and, after the family moved to Pennsylvania, the youngest daughter, who was named Philadelphia.

At no time in Dolly's life was she known by her proper Christian name. According to a family legend, William could not pronounce Dorothea and called his baby sister Dolly. Many older people and members of her own generation spelled the name Dolley, and some, among them Thomas Jefferson, showed no favoritism by spelling it both ways.

Virginia gentry were careful to follow English traditions, and the Paynes were no exception, so Dolly and her sisters were tutored at home. Their principal teacher was a poor spinster, a distant relative, who taught them to read, write, and "do sums." Dolly also acquired a smattering of the classics. The same tutor also taught a cousin on her father's side, Dorothea Dandridge, another great beauty, who would achieve her own renown by rejecting the ardent suit of the great naval hero of the American Revolution, John Paul Jones, instead becoming the happily contented second wife of Governor Patrick Henry, whose eldest daughter by his deceased first wife was her closest friend.

Several enthusiastic nineteenth-century ladies who wrote biographies of Dolly insisted she was something of an intellectual, but neither her own letters nor the many observations written about her during her life substantiate this claim. It is true that after she married James Madison she picked up enough French to converse haltingly in that language with Jefferson, who had lived in Paris for years, but by her own admission her husband's attempt to teach her Latin failed because of her "negligence." Most of Madison's political treatises were too deep for her, and there is no evidence to suggest that the Father of the Constitution made his bride familiar with the great document to which he had contributed so much seven years before their marriage.

One learned to be a lady by emulating one's elders, and Grandmother Coles, with whom Dolly and her sisters spent their summers and many other holidays, set a shining example. From her the little girl acquired a fascination with the preparation of food and an appreciation of fabrics and style in clothing. Until the end of her own life Dolly frequently spoke of a "transparent silken cap" that her grandmother wore over her own hair, and it would inspire the design of the "Dolly Madison headgear" that would become the rage of the United States and Europe. Grandmother Coles also taught the little girl how to treat servants with consideration and the art of putting one's guests at ease. Her grandmother, Dolly later said, was the single most important influence during her formative years.

The Payne family often visited Dolly's uncle, Colonel John Coles, whose Albemarle County plantation house was a gathering place for young men who would later become leaders of their country during and after the Revolution. Three would become Presidents of the United States, and Dolly would marry one of them. She was acquainted with James Madison from her earliest childhood, but no records indicate that he paid any attention to a little girl seventeen years his junior. According to a rumor that was never denied, Thomas Jefferson had been attentive to Mary Coles before her marriage to John Payne. He was fond of her eldest children, and occasionally Walter, William, and Dolly, mounted on ponies from the Coles stable, accompanied him on rides through the nearby woods. Another young lawyer who often came to the plantation was Patrick Henry, who brought his ailing wife with him. This gaunt, intense man sometimes relaxed in the company of children, treating Dolly and her brothers to bedtime stories.

James Monroe was one of the younger visitors to Colonel Coles's estate, and may have known Dolly better at that time than did any of the other future leaders of the nation. During his first term as President, he revealed that the little girl, something of a tomboy because of her brothers' influence, habitually challenged him to foot races. Fairness compelled him to give her a handicap, he said, and not until many years later was she actually able to beat him in a race. Subsequently, as a matron, she continued to enjoy the sport, but her dignity forced her to compete only with members of her own sex.

In 1779, when Dolly was eleven, her father bought Scotchtown because he needed a large dwelling for his rapidly increasing family. The house was enormous. Built in 1732 by a Scotsman, it was 100 feet long and 50 feet deep, with an "English basement" of brick and the rest of clapboard. A number of rooms were paneled in oak, mahogany, or walnut and a tunnel in the entrance hall led to the so-called dungeon in the cellar, a chamber quickly appropriated by the children as a place to play without adult interference.

Later in life Dolly vividly recalled many features of Scotchtown. She shared a green-and-white bedroom with Lucy, eighteen months her junior, and the day-to-day activities of the girls were supervised by a slave called Mother Amy. At Dolly's insistence, Mother Amy was given her freedom when the family moved to Philadelphia, but she remained in Dolly's employ all her life.

Dolly learned to sew in what was known as the Blue

Room, where she was also admitted when company came to the house. The elder children usually sat in a corner, and they were expected to remain silent in the presence of guests. There, as a preadolescent, Dolly learned the manners and observed the social amenities that were to guide her. In two corners of the large chamber were fireplaces with black mantels, which the original owner had brought with him from Scotland. As an adult, Dolly remembered them with such fondness that she twice tried to purchase them, but in vain.

The lawns and gardens occupied the better part of an acre, and Dolly became an enthusiastic gardener. She learned to plant and weed, and developed a fondness for shrubs and boxwood that later enabled her to make the gardens of the Madison home a showplace. Unlike many of her contemporaries, who were content to "supervise" the work in their gardens, she enjoyed laboring on her hands and knees. Her attitude, remarkable in a Southerner of the period, was that the servants were her equals, and she expected nothing of them that she was unwilling to do herself. Actually, she worked harder than anyone else in the garden, a habit that stayed with her for more than sixty years.

In spite of the many luxuries Dolly enjoyed as a child, life on an eighteenth-century Virginia plantation was primitive. Indoor toilets were unknown, and the girls of the family used their own outhouse as well as chamber pots. There was no running water, and children were expected to wash in cold water drawn from a spring, regardless of the season. In order to minimize cooking odors and reduce the fire hazard, all cooking was done in a kitchen separate from the main house, which meant that many dishes cooled and sometimes congealed before being served. Candles, with the exception of exorbitantly expensive French tapers that were imported from Paris on rare occasions, smoked heavily and filled the rooms with a rancid smell. Thanks to innumerable drafts the rooms were icy in winter. They were also stifling in summer, and since screening was unknown, people were plagued by flies, mosquitoes, and gnats.

The principal meal of the day was taken late in the afternoon, and even when no company appeared, the courses often seemed endless. Stewed fruit came first, followed by soup. Fresh fish was served often, but the main course usually consisted of several dishes, including beef, ham or pork, roast fowl, or wild game, accompanied by side dishes of vegetables. Dessert might consist of several kinds of pies, tarts, and cakes. The rich Virginia soil produced almost anything on demand, but salads were virtually unknown in Virginia, as was also the case in the other colonies. Only those who lived near saltwater ate shellfish.

Most plantations, and that of John Payne, Jr., was no exception, were almost self-sustaining, a condition that remained unchanged after Dolly married James Madison. Housewives ordinarily were required to purchase only a few staples, among them wheat flour, sugar, tea, and a far less popular beverage, coffee.

Flax was grown on most farms, too, so linen was available in quantity, and most plantation owners raised sheep for their wool. Lamb and mutton were regarded as dishes fit only for lower-class city dwellers. The ginning of cotton was still a slow, laborious process done by hand; so little of it was grown in the South then that only small quantities were available for clothing. Shirts of a fine-spun cotton known as lawn were within reach of only the wealthy, as were silks and velvets.

Mary Payne was indifferent to her wardrobe, but her eldest daughter was spoiled by both of her clothes-conscious grandmothers, and she early in life gained an appreciation of such expensive fabrics as corduroy, velvet, and a mixture of linen and silk. At no time in her life did Dolly wear linsey-woolsey, the homespun material in which ordinary Americans customarily dressed.

Behind the main buildings of the plantation were the stables, the blacksmith's shop, and a cluster of other buildings. One was occupied for only a week or two each year, when an itinerant bootmaker came for a visit and made shoes of cowhide and deerskin that had been tanned on the property. Another building was the carpenter's shop, where most of the family's furniture was made. Yet another building housed the hooper. Spinning wheels were located in their own quarters, and on the larger estates soap and candles were made in a special pit located far enough from the main house to avoid the danger of fire.

Discipline in the Payne Quaker household was strict, and Dolly wore plain clothes, dressing in more elegant attire only when visiting one or the other of her grandmothers. All jewelry was forbidden, and she was compelled to hide beneath her unadorned dress a gold locket and chain given her by Grandmother Coles. She was never allowed to forget she was a lady, and when she went outdoors, she was compelled to wear gloves to protect her hands, a sunbonnet, and a linen mask that prevented the appearance of "ugly freckles."

After the family moved to Scotchtown she was no longer tutored at home, but accompanied Walter and William to the Quaker School, which was so well attended that two classrooms were used. The same subjects were taught in both, and the curriculum was confined to the rudiments. Boys who, because of their family position and wealth, would go on to college at the age of fourteen or fifteen received private tutoring at home in Latin, the classics, philosophy, mathematics, and theology. Girls were given no opportunity to study these advanced subjects.

Dolly, who was a conscientious student, did not rebel

openly against the inferior position automatically assigned to members of her sex, and the idea of demanding equal treatment probably did not occur to her. Nevertheless, she preferred the company of her older brothers to that of her younger sisters, and often went fishing with them, a pastime she continued to enjoy as an adult, much to the surprise of friends, who regarded such outings as beneath the dignity of a lady.

Her brothers taught her to handle pistols, and on one occasion, when she was twelve, she went hunting with them in the woods near Scotchtown. Girls were not allowed to participate in such a dangerus sport, and her shocked parents "chastised" her. The nature of her punishment is unknown. Presumably she was confined to her room for a period of twenty-four to forty-eight hours, and it is unlikely that she was spanked with a birch rod, a form of discipline reserved for unruly boys.

She rode daily, having graduated from ponies to horses, and in spite of her mother's remonstrances she continued to run foot races, often competing with the children of slaves as well as with her siblings and friends.

No portraits of Dolly were painted until she reached her twenties, but she was considered a beauty from the time of her birth. Cousin Patrick Henry, writing in January, 1769, called her a "lovely" infant, and countless others used the same adjective to describe her for the next eighty years. She grew to medium height, which in the late eighteenth century was about five feet two inches, and was always inclined to be plump. Slenderness was not regarded favorably in the period, and her rounded face and figure were universally admired.

Thanks to her rigid Quaker upbringing, however, Dolly did not think of her appearance as an asset. She accepted her beauty without question, as she did the color of her eyes and hair, and she shrugged off the compliments she received for her physical attributes. Some of her contemporaries regarded her as exceptionally modest, but they failed to understand her approach to the subject. She took her beauty for granted and was surprised when others were dazzled by it.

There is no indication that she longed for the company of the great or wanted to play a role in history. Because her place in the social hierarchy was secure, she was not impressed by titles or high rank. Early in life she learned to evaluate and enjoy people as individuals, no matter what positions they held. Only those who knew her best ever realized that this attitude was responsible for her unique triumphs.

II

*D*olly Payne stood on the threshold of her seventh birthday when the American War of Independence broke out in April, 1775. It is unlikely that the conflict made any great impression on her at that time. As a member of an ardent Patriot family, however, she must have been conscious of many developments through the years.

Cousin Patrick Henry, who shared responsibility with Samuel Adams of Boston for awakening the American people to a yearning for independence from Britain, was a frequent visitor to his former home, and he continued to visit Dolly's parents when he was serving as governor of Virginia. His successor, Thomas Jefferson, was a close friend of John and Mary Payne, and he brought his attractive young wife to Scotchtown on many occasions. The older children were allowed to dine with guests and to join the adults in the parlor, provided they were "seen but not heard," and as the war undoubtedly was the principal topic of conversation, Dolly had ample opportunity to learn a great deal.

On at least one occasion, in the autumn of 1779, the twenty-eight-year-old James Madison dined at Scotchtown. Already recognized as a legislator and administrator, he had served as a prewar member of the Virginia

Committee of Public Safety, been one of the framers of the state constitution, and been elected to the House of Burgesses. For almost two years a member of the Council of State, the governor's cabinet, he soon would become a delegate to the Continental Congress. Madison was short, slender, and physically agile, with a high forehead and sharply defined features that made him look older than his age.

A serious student of law, philosophy, and theology, Madison was believed to be lacking a sense of humor, a conviction that would grow as he became increasingly prominent. The charge, fortified by the natural dignity that made it difficult for him to unbend in public, was false, and even as a child Dolly must have known it.

During his visit Madison rode with the elder Payne children, built a bonfire for them, and sang with them, even though he could not carry a tune. Whether the eleven-year-old girl could appreciate his quiet jokes, usually sophisticated puns and other plays on words, is open to question. Romantic writers of the late nineteenth century said Dolly was drawn to him and that he could see the future belle in her, but these claims have no substance in known fact. It is enough that they were acquainted and at no time met as strangers. The only significance to be found in their relationship during this period is that they had similar backgrounds. Both were members of the tiny, educated, estate-owning class from which so many of Virginia's and the nation's leaders were drawn in the first half century of American independence.

By 1781, when Dolly was thirteen, she had to be ever conscious of the war. Walter was serving with the Virginia militia as a captain, and William, who had threatened to run away in order to join the Continentals, had been kept at home only by a parental promise that he would be allowed to enlist on his sixteenth birthday.

Virginia had seen relatively little of the war, but now it became an active theater, due in large part to one of the most competent and ruthless of British commanders. Colonel Banastre Tarleton was a cavalryman who regarded the eighteenth-century concept of chivalry as outmoded. Enemy capacities to wage war should be destroyed, he believed, and he acted accordingly. Leading a brigade consisting of his own regiment and several troops of Loyalist irregulars, he ranged through Virginia, burning crops, confiscating the food gathered in barns and warehouses, and creating havoc everywhere. Martha Washington, wife of the American commander-in-chief, felt uneasy at her Mount Vernon plantation. Governor Jefferson deemed it expedient to move his wife and daughters from their Monticello home to a safer place.

The Paynes, like so many other Patriots, made plans to evacuate their plantations without delay if Tarleton's raiders were reported in the area. Grains and vegetables were sold as soon as they were harvested; tobacco, the money crop, was sent westward in carts and wagons to hiding places in the mountains. These efforts to ward off disaster were difficult for Virginia's patricians to make. Ever since the founding of the Jamestown colony in 1607, the aristocrats of Britain had been the models on whom Virginia's leaders had constructed their own society. Now Tarleton and his officers were regarded as heartless plunderers, murderers, and rapists, barbarians of an even lower order than the mercenary troops the British hired from the German states, because as officers they should have known better. The Virginians felt the British had abandoned the code of gentlemen. That they themselves were no longer regarded as gentry by the British was as irrelevant to them as it was beyond their credence.

Some families succumbed so completely to panic that their carpenters, hoopers, and tanners made chastity belts for the ladies of the household. The Paynes were more sensible, so Dolly, unlike some of her school friends, was not subjected to the indignity of being forced to wear a clumsy contraption made of leather, wood, and metal. In fact, her parents were able to rise above the hysteria, and their broad-minded approach made it possible for their eldest daughter to adopt a realistic attitude, too. Neither the threat of an invasion by Tarleton's bogeymen nor the far more serious incident in which Dolly was involved as First Lady during the War of 1812 made her anti-British. She could entertain visiting nobles, members of Parliament, and other distinguished Britons with a charm and aplomb that were genuine. Early in life, in a manner unknown to posterity, she learned to treat people as individuals and refused to cripple them with belittling ethnic or national labels.

General Washington's victory over the army of General Lord Cornwallis at Yorktown, Virginia, in 1781 ensured American independence, even though fighting continued in the South until the signing of the peace treaty in 1783. The approach of peace enabled John and Mary Payne to survey their own long-range future, and they were unhappy with what they saw. Their plantation was no longer profitable. They could no longer afford tutors, and the neighborhood school was providing their children with an inadequate education. Worst of all, the family's finances depended on the institution of slavery, which they opposed.

John Payne then conceived the idea of moving to Philadelphia, the principal center of Quaker activity in the new United States, and late in 1781 he visited Pennsylvania to evaluate the possibility of establishing a new home there. His wife went with him, as did Dolly, the only one of the children privileged to make the trip.

There were no roads worthy of the name south of Maryland, and the Paynes had to make the first part of their journey on horseback, stopping overnight at the homes of friends and relatives. Until they reached the Potomac River Dolly traveled through countryside similar to that which she knew. The horses followed trails through wooded areas, emerging into the open on public lands adjacent to estates where tobacco was the principal crop.

But when the trio crossed the state line into Maryland and transferred to a public stage, there was an abrupt change. Farms were much smaller, towns were large and still growing, and small factories began to appear, most of them boasting only a handful of employees. The coach made frequent stops, none of them scheduled, to discharge and take on passengers. The horses were changed frequently at taverns, where grilled meats were the staple of every meal. Overnight halts were made at inns, where as many as six to twelve people crowded into each bedroom. When possible, ladies were given preferential treatment and were granted a small measure of privacy, which meant that the girl shared a bed with her mother and father.

Philadelphia, the seat of the Continental Congress, was the official capital of the United States, and was still the largest city in the country. Its population of 45,000 exceeded that of Boston by about 10,000, and it was twice the size of New York Town. Certainly it must have been a bewildering metropolis to an adolescent who had never before left Virginia or visited any community of consequence.

Armed privateers, most of them flying the pennant of the Pennsylvania navy, were anchored beside 42-gun French frigates and other warships. Merchantmen from Holland, Spain, and Sweden lined the wharves, as did coastal trading vessels from New England and the West Indian islands. The docks were piled high with kegs of rum and barrels of molasses, bolts of cloth and kitchen ironware, boxes of tea and hogsheads of carpenters' tools, all of them en route to mammoth warehouses that held thousands of tons of merchandise. Elsewhere were mountains of lumber, America's principal export, awaiting stacking in the holds of the brigs and sloops. Seamen spoke many languages as they roamed the waterfront, and the area was honeycombed with taverns where sailors could find liquor and girls.

Ladies never tarried in this district, so it is likely that Dolly was driven past the produce market, the most extensive in the Western Hemisphere, to the more sedate sections of the city. By her own later admission she gaped at the rows of shops that sold cloth and food, books, shoes, and even such items as candles and soap, which Virginians made at home. The streets were filled with horsemen and carriages and carts, the streets themselves were cobbled, and pedestrians moved in all directions.

Among them were ladies and gentlemen in the latest French styles, many of them wigged, as well as farmers in homespun and Indians in greasy leather. "In my first thirty minutes in Philadelphia," Dolly said a generation later, "I saw more people than I had observed in all of my previous life."

Unlike Boston and New York, where many inns were maintained for the convenience of travelers, Philadelphia specialized in the more homelike atmosphere of lodging houses. There visitors not only took suites, which boasted private parlors for the entertainment of friends, but also ate most of their meals, since there were few taverns catering to the gentry. Delegates to the Congress and high-ranking officers from each state usually banded together, so there were places favored by every state. John Payne had made his arrangements for accommodations well in advance, and his wife and daughter found that most of their fellow lodgers were old friends and neighbors from Virginia. One of the first to call was James Madison, who lived nearby, but it is unlikely that he paid much attention to the daughter of his friends.

Payne, aided by Virginians and members of the Quaker community, explored possible ways to earn a living, and meanwhile his wife and daughter went house hunting for their large, still-growing family. Dolly was fascinated by the clothes she saw, and although Quaker practice forbade extravagance, she exerted her charm sufficiently to persuade her parents to buy her a length of dark-green silk, woven in France. Eventually it was made into a modest gown of her own design, and she wore it for years, the first item in a wardrobe so extensive that she would be regarded as a fashion leader whose influence was exceeded only by that of Napoleon's first wife, the Empress Josephine.

John and Mary Payne returned to Virginia, reluctant to make a move that would force them to change their whole way of life, but their eldest daughter did not share their hesitation. Dolly had sampled the sophistication of a city, and she was hungry for an entire meal. She wanted to move as soon as possible and, in her enthusiasm, spoke of little else.

Her parents ultimately reached the conclusion that they had to make the move, and began the tedious task of packing their household belongings, which would be shipped by water. John Payne took the drastic step of granting his slaves their freedom, a gesture made in accordance with a principle in which he believed, and which cost him a large sum. Mother Amy, the cook, and two housemaids agreed to accompany the family as freedwomen. The continuing presence of four servants under the Payne roof did not necessarily mean the family's financial condition was sound. Experienced domestic help, particularly a nursemaid or cook, received no more than fifty cents per week in wages, in addition to room, meals, and clothing.

Dolly was old enough, at thirteen, to know city life would not be perfect and that she would have to make sacrifices. The horses were being sold, so she could no longer go on a daily canter across the fields. There were no woods through which she could walk and daydream. Living space would be cramped, so it was probable she would have to share a bedroom with two of her sisters rather than one. And her mother made it clear that she would be expected to play a greater role in the management and supervision of the younger children.

In spite of these handicaps, however, she was eager to meet the challenge. A young lady reared in the eighteenth century was prepared for only one future, that of a wife, and Dolly knew that Philadelphia was a magnet for America's most important, wealthy, and powerful men.

III

The Payne family moved from Virginia to Philadelphia in May, 1783, the month when Dolly turned fifteen, and accomplished the two-hundred-mile journey after spending five long days on the road. The peace treaty with Great Britain was signed about three months later, on September 3, and the United States entered a new era.

The euphoria that grew out of the mother country's recognition of American independence could not hide the new nation's many weaknesses from thinking men. She was financially exhausted after the long war and owed vast sums abroad, particularly to France. She was still an agricultural nation with few industries of her own, and continued to depend on others, Great Britain most of all, for her manufactured goods.

Her greatest weaknesses were political. The Congress was a forum for rhetorical exercise and lacked the strength to make its will felt. The concurrence of nine of the original thirteen states was necessary to establish any policy, and squabbles were endless, each state regarding the others as rivals. Under the Articles of Confederation that established the limits of the national government, most powers were retained by the states, which were reluctant to give up any.

For example, fiscal chaos threatened the country. Inflation was rampant, and the Continental paper dollar, issued without backing by the Congress throughout the war, had become virtually worthless. So each state issued its own money, and interstate trade and commerce suffered badly.

The nation's foreign affairs were equally muddled. The Westerners hated Spain, which interfered with American traffic on the region's lifeline to the sea, the Mississippi River. Most Americans still despised Britain, even though the farsighted realized that a sound economy depended upon the reestablishment of equitable trade relations with London. People were grateful to France for her help in winning the war, but the government of King Louis XVI was too weak itself to play a major role in the development of the new nation.

All the same, the three million citizens of the United States believed implicitly in their future, and they were determined to prove that their radical experiment in democratic government would succeed. Shipyards were busy again, building a vastly expanded merchant fleet. New factories, most of them manufacturing desperately needed consumer goods, were coming into being, especially in Massachusetts, Connecticut, New York, and Pennsylvania. The soil was rich, there were valuable minerals in the earth, and the trees in the forests, which stretched far beyond the country's hazily defined boundaries toward the distant Pacific Ocean, were uncounted and uncountable, the future source of dazzling wealth.

Land was the cause of America's optimism. Millions of unoccupied acres beckoned the poor of England and Ireland, Scotland and Wales, and to a lesser extent the impoverished of France, Sweden, and the German states. Land was the mirage that caused the townsman of the

Eastern Seaboard to migrate to the frontier. The lure of land was an irresistible tide. Vermont, which would become the fourteenth state in 1791, was already agitating for admission to the Union, and so was Kentucky. Pioneers in what would become Tennessee were too impatient to tolerate the inability of the Congress to take decisive action, and the inhabitants of the eastern portion of that territory had already formed their own state, which they called Franklin.

Everyone speculated in Western land. Robert Morris, the distinguished Philadelphia financier and banker, plunged so deeply into the market that, within a few years, he became bankrupt. General Washington, who had retired to his Virginia estate, was drawn into a scheme that envisaged the digging of a network of canals connecting the seaboard and the region beyond the mountains. Even Thomas Paine, the master propagandist, whose pen had been a major influence in the winning of the war, invested funds he could ill afford to risk in land companies that based their future on dreams rather than reality.

Only a handful, including James Madison of Virginia and Alexander Hamilton of New York, Washington's former aide-de-camp, believed the United States would be unable to live up to her promise until the states relinquished a portion of their authority to a strong national government. Few men heeded their warnings, however, so they were forced to wait until the nation floundered in the morass created by the Confederation.

Dolly Payne knew little and cared less about these grave matters of state. Life was too exciting for a girl who, in two more years, would be recognized as a grown woman. Her father wasn't too poor to buy a house in the most fashionable part of town, on Chestnut Street, and he paid two thousand dollars in cash for it, a staggering sum. It was a three-story frame building, painted white, and was considered small because it contained "only" eighteen rooms and was surrounded by a tiny yard. In a few years Dolly would confess that what impressed her was the fact that there were more than four thousand private houses in Philadelphia, the nation's best planned and most beautiful city, where there were many parks, handsome public buildings, and so many schools that a girl could become confused just trying to count them.

Dolly was entered in a Quaker school, as were her younger sisters and brothers, and she soon discovered that she was poorly prepared for the level of education to which she was exposed. Most subject matter was advanced far beyond what she had learned in Virginia, and she struggled dutifully but vainly in an attempt to catch up with others of her age. She spent a full year in school, but happily took advantage of the Quaker law that allowed her to leave when she reached her 16th birthday.

She was so friendly and warm that she encountered no difficulty in making friends within the confines of Quaker society, which engulfed the Paynes. Within a short time she was invited to many social functions given by and for her contemporaries, most of them early-evening affairs at which the adolescents played simple, innocent games. She attended no dances because members of the Society of Friends regarded dancing as too frivolous a pastime.

Dolly's later correspondence with some of her sisters hints that her appearance was a cause of concern for her parents and other adults of the Quaker community, and that some girls of her own age were troubled, too. She was exceptionally pretty by the standards of her time, her plump figure was maturing rapidly, and the boys—like those of any era—ogled her breasts. But it was her natural vivacity more than anything else that caused problems.

Dolly was a social creature who thoroughly enjoyed

(33)

the company of others, and, liking everyone, she did not differentiate between males and females. Her ultimate success as a hostess and her stature as a personality in her own right grew out of her genuine interest in people, regardless of sex, accomplishments, or position. Even at fifteen she was demonstrating a talent for establishing cordial relations with anyone she met, and she achieved instant popularity.

She had a magnetic quality that drew people to her, an attraction that a later age would call charisma. People were always aware of her proximity. Men stared at her when she and her schoolmates walked down the streets of Philadelphia, and so did women. At a social gathering she became the center of attention, although she made no effort to steal the limelight. Increasingly interested in clothes and fascinated by the French fabrics now on display in the city's shops, she still wore the drab attire favored by the Quakers, so it could not have been her clothes that made her the object of so much interest.

Inevitably, some of her classmates became jealous and complained, some speaking directly to her and others going to their own parents, who then had words with Mary Payne. It was not seemly, they said, for a girl active in the Society of Friends to flirt, encourage the attentions of males, and make a public spectacle of herself.

Dolly was upset and hurt by the unwarranted criticism. Mary Payne, who knew her daughter, refused to be influenced by what she regarded as unfair, and took the girl's part. Dolly was no flirt, she said, and made no conscious effort to call attention to herself. Her stand was echoed many years later, in 1808, when President Madison's enemies attacked him by claiming that his wife was a woman who was happy only when surrounded by men. No less a personage than former President Thomas Jefferson came to her immediate defense. Saying that he had known her since earliest childhood, he insisted he had never seen her flirt with anyone.

Encouraged by parental support, Dolly continued to go her own way and made no attempt to curb her natural exuberance. In time her disregard for the derogatory opinions of others became habitual. If she was sensitive to criticism, she learned to keep her feelings to herself, and never mentioned in her correspondence or elsewhere that she believed she had been wronged. Many people noted, after she became First Lady, that her attitudes were similar to Madison's. He, too, lived as he believed right, and his conscience remained untroubled when irresponsible abuse was heaped on him.

This approach to life was typical of eighteenth-century men and women of integrity, and neither Dolly nor Madison necessarily deserves admiration for taking it. Scurrilous assaults made on persons of prominence were commonplace. The only mass medium of public opinion was the press, which lacked influence and felt under no constraint to present facts accurately and fairly. It was enough for a man of dignity and stature to believe in himself.

Dolly made only a few enemies, it appears, and was popular with most of her peers, girls as well as boys. Young men beyond school age began to notice her, and their ranks included neophytes in business and politics who were not members of the Quaker community. Mary Payne discouraged them, however, indicating that her daughter was not yet old enough to take any suit seriously. Her firmness prevented the development of situations that might prove embarrasing to her daughter, and Dolly continued to live the relatively uncomplicated life of a schoolgirl.

Meanwhile, her parents were finding the transition to a new life far more difficult to achieve. The freeing of their slaves had been a costly gesture, even though their new friends and neighbors approved of it. Pennsylvania had abolished slavery in 1780, making it the first state to take such action. However, the combination of a virtually worthless Continental dollar and rampaging inflation made money tight, and John Payne's woes were complicated when he was forced to sell his Virginia estate for less than he had hoped to receive. In spite of the optimism inspired by the mere mention of land, real estate values in the older, settled regions of the country were declining.

Had Payne been more experienced in finance he might have guessed that his failure to sell Scotchtown for the price he wanted was an indication that the land bubble in the West was going to burst. Instead he joined all the others who were investing in the region beyond the mountains, and put every penny he could scrape together into a company that was buying a huge tract in the fertile Ohio Valley, to which immigrants and impoverished American townspeople were moving by the thousands.

Meantime he needed immediate cash income to support his family. The country was suffering from many shortages in the days following the close of the war, and Payne decided to open a small factory that would manufacture starch, which was almost impossible to obtain in the Middle Atlantic states. By a simple process, the substance could be extracted from corn, potatoes, wheat, and other grains and vegetables, and the market was ready-made.

Unfortunately the former Virginian had spent his entire life in farming and knew no other vocation. He spent too much on his plant and equipment, hired too many workers, and paid too high a price for his raw materials. His mistakes taught him painful lessons that forced him to change his practices, but by then a number of competitors in both Pennsylvania and New Jersey had entered the field, and he faced a constant struggle to remain solvent. At no time did his enterprise show a profit, and each year he was compelled to take funds from his dwindling reserves in order to keep it afloat.

His investment in Ohio Valley land fared no better. The deeds of the company proved faulty, and three others were claiming the same tract, a common occurrence in a time when few organizers had actually visited the West and seen the land they believed they owned.

Lawsuits proliferated, and local favoritism was rampant. Four states—Massachusetts, Connecticut, New York, and Pennsylvania—were claiming portions of the Ohio Valley as extensions of their own domains, and the courts of each were openly partial to the citizens of their own states. A New Yorker was almost certain to win a verdict in a New York court, but it proved impossible to enforce that ruling, and the conflicts in legal judgments made the confusion worse.

While the investors squabbled, the newcomers from the British Isles and the poor of the East Coast who had gone west for cheap land took matters into their own hands. They quickly discovered that frontiersmen made their own laws, and that by cutting down trees, building cabins, and tilling the soil they established squatters' rights. Once a man had laid claim to a homestead in Ohio and actually had settled there, it was almost beyond the power of a court in Philadelphia, Hartford, or Boston to oust him from the property.

In 1786 the land company in which John Payne had put all of his "spare" capital went bankrupt. It was just one of many companies to suffer that fate, and there was literally nothing a disappointed speculator could do to protect his supposed rights or obtain redress for his alleged grievances. Payne, like so many others, had nothing to show for his money except a handsomely embossed sheet of parchment.

Expenses were far greater in Philadelphia, where it was necessary to purchase food and clothing for a large family, than they had been on a virtually self-sufficient plantation in Virginia. Payne and his wife saw their capital shrinking rapidly and were forced to retrench.

The two eldest Payne sons were earning their own way in the world, but seven children still lived at home. Dolly, the eldest of them, was given the greatest responsibility, and she was so busy it was as well that she left school in 1784, when she was sixteen. The former slave who had accompanied the family to Philadelphia as a cook died that same year, and since the cost of another servant at Philadelphia's inflated wage scale of one dollar per week was beyond the limits of the Payne budget, Dolly became the chief cook.

Her mother went to the market on Tuesdays and Fridays, when the ringing of church bells announced the arrival of fresh meats, fish, poultry, and produce. Lucy, who was now fourteen, and the other younger girls cleaned the food and washed dishes after a meal, but it was Dolly who tended the hot pots on the open hearth in the kitchen and actually prepared the food.

The menus served by Dolly Madison in later years won her such renown that she was known as America's finest cook, and anyone to whom she gave a recipe treasured it. When complimented, she often answered that she experimented in the kitchen because she found cooking a boring pastime, and her guests laughed politely, believing she was making the modest reply expected under the circumstances.

The truth was that Dolly *was* bored in the kitchen. The fascination of cooking that had caused her to "help" in her grandmother's Coles Hill kitchen as a little girl gave way to ennui when she was forced to prepare three meals every dreary day for a family of nine. She overcame the monotony of the chore by inventing and experimenting with new dishes, and she proved herself imaginatively adept. The diplomats and statesmen who believed that Dolly Madison was subjected to French influences in her preparation of meals were mistaken. She neither visited France nor engaged a French chef, and only Americans cooked in the taverns where she infrequently dined.

The Payne family was in the first financial bind that any member had ever known, and Dolly proved equal to the challenge. She learned to cook inexpensive cuts of meat over low fires for long periods in order to make them tender, and she was particularly good at using leftovers and meat bones in her many soups. Few items cost less at the market than West Indian sugar, at ten pounds for a penny, so she became expert at making and decorating sweet tarts, which were especially popular with the younger children.

Whether she wrote down most of her recipes over the years or merely remembered them is unknown. If reduced to paper, they vanished and were lost to posterity. Some genuine Dolly Madison recipes still exist, of course, but it is difficult and perhaps impossible to distinguish the genuine from the spurious. Dolly suffered from the George-Washington-slept-here syndrome adopted in later times by so many inns on the Eastern Seaboard, and countless recipes are attributed to her. Even if she had spent her entire life in the kitchen, it is unlikely that she could have developed more than a fraction of them.

While living under the roof of her Quaker parents, it is unlikely that Dolly used alcoholic beverages in her cooking. Jefferson, whose interests were eclectic, returned from France with a taste for wine cooking, and discussed its secrets with her when, as the wife of his Secretary of State, she acted as his official hostess. During Jefferson's first term as President, from 1800 to 1804, Dolly's recipes became more sophisticated. It is a sign of her free-wheeling skill that she not only utilized various wines, but concocted recipes that utilized whiskey, rum, and applejack, all of them products of the Western Hemisphere.

She also had ample opportunity to utilize and expand

her skills as a seamstress. Her mother, who had taught her to sew, still made some of the younger children's clothing, and Mother Amy did most of the mending, but soon after moving to Philadelphia Dolly began to make her own dresses. Later she designed and made many for Lucy, too.

She suffered from a number of seemingly insurmountable handicaps. The Society of Friends frowned on French silks and velvets, most of which anyhow were far too expensive for John Payne's budget. But Dolly had a real interest in clothes, and as her talents increased, she became ingenious in her creative designs. Yearning for gowns of rich material that were beyond her parents' means and outside the pale of the circles in which she moved, she nevertheless found ways to gratify at least some of her desires.

Occasionally she could buy remnants and scraps of expensive fabrics. She came to know a number of the merchants who imported such goods and haunted their shops. Soon she was making gores and panel collars and facings of dark silk or velvet. She blended these materials into the somber costumes with such skill that neither her parents nor their Quaker friends could protest.

For years the fashionable ladies of France and England had been wearing dresses with daringly low-cut bosoms and tight-fitting bodices. Dolly knew her own figure was superior to that of any wealthy lady she saw on the streets of Philadelphia, but she also realized she would not be permitted to wear gowns that revealing. So she compromised, going as far as she could in her designs while remaining within the boundaries of taste approved by the Quaker community. Eyebrows may have been raised in silence, but no records indicate that anyone protested aloud, so the young designer-seamstress persisted in her efforts.

Dolly may have felt frustrated during this early stage of her amateur career as a dressmaker, but she later knew the worth of her difficult apprenticeship. Her imagination became disciplined, and she learned to harness it within the boundaries of good taste. Yet, at the same time, she could create a new style that would be copied with enthusiasm in both North America and Europe. Far more than her personal beauty was responsible for her emergence as a leader of feminine style, and although the high post James Madison eventually won helped her to step into the spotlight, even that was secondary. Her skills were so great that she would have risen to the top in any age.

IV

$\mathcal{B}$y 1787 the infant United States was floundering, her affairs chaotic. Relations with other countries were crumbling, she was unable to utilize the wealth of her natural resources to climb from the pit of approaching bankruptcy, and people everywhere were increasingly discontented. The West continued to grow, but the sectional and individual jealousies of the states, combined with their sharply conflicting claims, still blocked the admission of new states to the Union.

Men of substance who had devoted their lives and fortunes to the establishment of the independent republic in the New World had invested heavily in the bonds, issued by the Congress, that had kept the nation afloat. Now they faced personal disaster, and the covetous in Great Britain were awaiting the opportunity to restore the one-time Colonies to their former status.

Patrick Henry of Virginia, Samuel Adams of Massachusetts, and some of the other fiery rebels who had led the country into the American Revolution still maintained that the rights of the separate states were paramount, that liberty would survive only through a form of government similar to the Confederation. Most of those who had been associated with them before and during the war disagreed, however, and so did the younger leaders who were becoming more prominent.

A majority, including those who still wanted to guard the rights of the states, felt that the nation would survive and prosper only if the form of government was altered and a more powerful national government established. Madison and Hamilton had been indefatigable in trying to set up a stronger, more perfect government, and the inability of the Congress to persuade the states to amend the Articles of Confederation added weight to their arguments.

The voices of the most influential and respected men in the United States began to be heard. General Washington wrote that it was imperative to give greater power to a central government, and so did the conservative John Adams of Massachusetts, who was abroad, as was Jefferson, another advocate. The aged Benjamin Franklin agreed with this stand, and prominent men in all of the states except Rhode Island, which was not represented, sent delegates to attend a Constitutional Convention in Philadelphia.

The Virginia delegation was headed by Governor Edmund Randolph. Madison, who was thirty-six at the time and still a bachelor, had done a great deal of advance work on a new constitution for the country, working in concert with his fellow Virginian, George Mason, as well as with Alexander Hamilton of New York, John Dickinson of Delaware, and Roger Sherman of Connecticut. Washington, who had announced his intention of attending as an "ordinary" member of the Virginia delegation, was thwarted in that aim. The most highly regarded of Americans, his mere presence at the Convention was a guarantee to citizens everywhere that this was no fly-by-night group intent on the destruction of men's liberties.

The Convention assembled on May 25, 1787, a scant five days after Dolly Payne's nineteenth birthday. Although her interest in politics was minimal and she probably had little knowledge of the state of the Union, she could not have failed to know that the meeting was taking place. It is unlikely, however, that she agreed with Jefferson's later assessment to the effect that the Convention was an "assemblage of demi-gods." The gentlemen who came to call on her parents in the rambling old house on Chestnut Street were old friends of the family, and she was in awe of no one.

When General Washington came to the Payne house, he singled out Dolly for attention because his wife was fond of her, having known the girl through some of her own relatives, members of the Custis family. Madison, who could think only of the Constitution, saw Dolly when he called, but she appears to have made no impression on him. Nor was she drawn to the intense, balding little man who could not sit in one place and paced the length of her parents' parlor, somehow balancing a cup of hot tea in one hand.

Dolly's broadest dimpled smile was reserved for Dr. Franklin, a lifelong admirer of attractive girls who had relished his avocation during his years as minister to France. He walked with the aid of a stick and was inclined to nap during the sessions of the Convention after drinking French wine with his meals. His eyesight was failing, too, but he could still see well enough when he wished, and peering at Dolly through the bifocals he had invented so many years earlier, he issued a typical Franklin pronouncement.

"You," he said in a high-pitched, quavering voice that nevertheless carried to every corner of the crowded parlor, "are the most beautiful young lady in America, and I've never met your equal in Paris or London."

Dolly received countless compliments over the years, but Dr. Franklin's accolade stood apart from all the rest, and she was fond of quoting it verbatim a half century later. "Benjamin Franklin," she sometimes added, "was a man of great charm." Apparently she never knew that he made similar observations to other girls.

Members of the Virginia delegation continued to drop in at the Payne home during the weeks the Convention deliberated. Madison, whose contributions of substance to the new Constitution were greater than those of any other man and who worked unceasingly to reconcile the differences that separated the groups from various states, was a frequent visitor, finding temporary relief from his burdens in the company of old friends.

He continued to be blind to Dolly's beauty, however, and her warm personality failed to impress him. Certainly he knew the work in which he was engaged was of paramount importance to the future of the United States, so it may be that he was impervious to the charms of even the prettiest of girls. Dolly seems to have remained indifferent to him, too, and if she developed an admiration for him, she succeeded in concealing her feelings from her contemporaries, as well as from future generations. He was a family acquaintance, nothing else, and they developed no close relationship.

The nineteenth-century ladies who wrote in such glowing terms about the romance between Dolly and Madison loved to dwell on this period, saying they became close friends who understood and learned to appreciate each other. But no known facts bear out this sentimental contention. Madison was a hard-pressed, busy man whose thoughts and energies were concentrated on a monumental task, and Dolly had no reason to spark to him. No attraction, chemical or otherwise, drew them to each other, and the better part of a decade would pass before they became intimate. So much for romance in 1787.

Many eighteenth-century girls were married by the time they reached nineteen, and a number of Dolly's classmates had already found husbands. She had no lack of eligible suitors, and the young bachelors of Philadelphia paid frequent visits to the Payne house to pay court to her and to seventeen-year-old Lucy, who was also exceptionally attractive. Dolly was friendly with all and encouraged none, deftly avoiding entanglements. She appears to have deferred any thoughts of marriage she may have entertained because she was needed at home.

Her father's starch factory was still losing money, and his faith in his ability to support his family was shaken. His capital was shrinking so rapidly that it would be exhausted in a few years, and Dolly discussed the situation frankly in a letter to the eldest of her brothers, Walter, now living and working in Richmond. His reply was blunt. He knew of no way to solve the family's financial problems and was afraid they were condemned to years of scrimping.

The situation was complicated by Mary Payne's fragile health. She was exhausted after giving birth to twelve children, nine of them living, and was suffering from a rheumatic condition that made walking difficult for her. More than ever, Dolly was needed at home, to supervise the activities of the younger children and to act as housekeeper. She accepted the burden cheerfully, without complaint, having been reared to believe that duty took precedence over one's personal desires. Neither she nor Lucy thought seriously of trying to escape from unpleasantness at home by marrying. Loyalty to family was a necessity that a young lady of breeding never questioned, no matter what her aspirations or dreams might tempt her to do.

In 1789 "Mr. Madison's Constitution" was duly ratified by the states and went into effect, creating a new federal government with executive, legislative, and judicial branches, each with its own duties and responsibilities. Amendments known as the Bill of Rights were added, and George Washington was elected President with John

Adams as Vice President. New York, the fastest-growing city in the country, with a population already greater than that of Boston, was selected as the first capital.

The new Congress was scheduled to meet on March 4, but travel was so slow that too few members were on hand. The House of Representatives finally convened on April 1, and the formation of a quorum enabled the Senate to gather on April 6. President Washington was inaugurated on April 30 and, in his two terms, held the office for a total of seven years and ten months.

Madison sought a seat in the Senate, but Richard Henry Lee and William Grayson were elected from Viriginia, so he ran for a place in the House. He was opposed by his good friend and neighbor, James Monroe, whose views on policy were similar to his own, and Madison was elected without difficulty.

From the outset he assumed a place of leadership in the House of Representatives, and it is significant that it was he who introduced nine of the ten Amendments to the Constitution that would make up the Bill of Rights. At the Constitutional Convention he had tried in vain to abolish the institution of slavery, which he despised, and he continued to agitate for the prompt emancipation of all slaves.

He was a strong supporter of Jefferson, who became Secretary of State, and after the Federalist party, which was formed by Hamilton, took root in New England and New York, he became active in the formation of the Jeffersonian Republican-Democratic party. President Washington refused to afflliate himself with either group, and so the political parties, for which the Constitution had made no provision, did not yet become a dominant force in American politics. Over a period of several years the Republican-Democrats gradually assumed the role of the loyal opposition, and Madison, in effect, became their leader in the House.

He had already achieved greater fame in the North

than in his native Virginia, which was slow to recognize his talents. Few people anywhere were aware of the decisive role he had played in drawing up the Constitution. The deliberations of the Convention had not been made public, and Madison's exhaustive notes on these sessions, which have been the principal source of information on the subject, were not published until the middle of the nineteenth century.

Madison's colleagues were conscious of his legal, administrative, and legislative abilities, but years would pass before the general public, in and out of Virginia, would know his real worth to the country. A great many people thought of him only as one of Jefferson's faithful lieutenants, and it did not yet occur to them that he was a man of extraordinary intellectual stature in his own right.

Whether Dolly Payne thought of him in any way is questionable. The capital of the country was moved from New York to Philadelphia in 1790, in part because it was more easily accessible from remote places and partly because its lodging houses offered more comfortable quarters to government officials. Madison may have called at the Payne home after his arrival, as he had done three years earlier, but there are no records to indicate that he paid any such visit to his old friends, much less to their daughter.

Dolly's life was unchanged by the move of the government, but her own situation was improving, and at last she could hope to be spared the stigma of spinsterhood. Mary Payne's physical condition had improved somewhat, enabling her to take a more active role in the management of household affairs, and most of her younger children were now old enough to look after themselves. Dolly was free to pursue her own interests, which were necessarily matrimonial in a time when no lady developed an independent career.

Women who read the novels of Daniel Defoe, Judge

Henry Fielding, and Laurence Sterne, the most popular authors of eighteenth-century fiction, would not have classified John Todd as a dashing, heroic type. By the standards of Philadelphia Quakers, however, there was no more eligible bachelor in all of Pennsylvania. He was twenty-five, a scant four years older than Dolly, and was earning a comfortable living as a lawyer. He was overweight, and a contemporary observed that his wooden false teeth were as conspicuous as those of President Washington. These minor handicaps to romance were more than overcome by his enthusiastic membership in the Society of Friends, which won him the support of John and Mary Payne in his campaign to win their eldest daughter's hand.

Dolly had other suitors who were more attractive physically and had livelier senses of humor, but her own common sense forced her to agree with her parents' evaluation of young Todd's assets. He was solvent, and had as many clients as he could handle. He already owned a house of his own at 83 Chestnut Street, only two blocks from the Payne home. He had little interest in politics, and consequently would spend most of his time attending to his own business interests. He was sober and conscientious, a man of obvious integrity, and best of all, he was so eager to marry Dolly that he was willing to waive the dowry her parents could ill afford to pay.

The whole family joined in the effort to persuade Dolly to accept Todd's suit. Her father, resigned to his own vocational ineptitude, was plaintive. Walter wrote to Dolly from Richmond, urging her not to lose this opportunity. The younger children surrounded Todd when he called, making their opinion of him clear. And Lucy, in what may have been a well-rehearsed confidential outburst, told her sister she would gladly accept Todd if Dolly didn't want him.

The question of love was beside the point. American

civilization may have been raw, but Old World attitudes still prevailed in the upper levels of society, and a girl married for security and social position. No matter what Dolly's inner feelings, she had no sensible replies to her family's eminently practical arguments. Early in January, 1790, she succumbed to their pleas.

The ecstatic Todd saw no reason why a long engagement should delay the winning of his prize, and the wedding took place on January 27 at the Friends Meeting House on Pine Street. The bride designed her own wedding gown, which she made in the Quaker tradition: it was modest, simple, and totally lacking in decoration. Relatives and other Quakers were in attendance, although it is not known whether any of the Virginians then in Philadelphia also were present.

The ceremony was brief. The bridal couple stood together on the women's side of the meetinghouse, and the groom said, "I, John Todd, do take thee, Dorothea Payne, to be my wedded wife, and promise, through Divine assistance, to be unto thee a loving husband, until separated by death."

Dolly made the same pledge, and was married. There was no music, the meetinghouse was bare of flowers, and no meal or reception followed the ceremony. Todd was strict in his observance of Quaker customs. The guests offered their felicitations, and the bridal couple drove in a rented carriage to the Todd house, where a newly hired pair of servants waited for them. The place was already furnished, so Dolly had no voice in its decoration.

Several months after Dolly's departure, her mother made drastic changes in the family's way of living. John Payne gave up all pretense of trying to earn a living as a starch maker, and his health declined rapidly. Lucy was married, and the next daughters, Anna and Mary, went off to boarding school, straining the family budget to the breaking point.

False pride was not one of Mary Payne's weaknesses, and she transformed her large home into a boardinghouse. One of the first to accept its hospitality was Secretary of State Jefferson, the senior member of the Cabinet, whose presence under the roof of his old friends gave the place a stature that no other dwelling in Philadelphia could achieve. His suite consisted of a parlor and bedroom.

The three Payne children who remained at home crowded into one room so more paying guests could be accommodated, and several members of the House of Representatives became boarders, meekly sleeping two to a room because the place was so crowded. Early in 1792 a new guest arrived, creating a considerable stir. He was Aaron Burr of New York, who had just defeated the old war hero, Major General Philip Schuyler, for a seat in the Senate. Schuyler was the father-in-law of Secretary of the Treasury Alexander Hamilton, who visited the house frequently in attempts to maintain a working relationship with the mercurial Burr, who was destined to kill him in the most notorious duel in American history.

Dolly's nineteenth-century biographers wrote that Congressman James Madison was a boarder at the Payne house during this period, and the story has survived to the present day. The tale is not true. When Dolly walked the short distance from her own small house to that of her parents, it is probable that, from time to time, she saw Jefferson. It may be that she sometimes also encountered Madison, who consulted often with the Secretary of State.

But such meetings, if they occurred, were casual. The Congressman from Virginia had no place in Dolly's full life; not only was she a married woman, trying to acclimate herself to the habits and home of her husband, but she was also pregnant.

V

On September 30, 1790, Dolly Todd gave birth to her first child, a son. Her mother and old Mother Amy were in attendance, as was a professional midwife. Philadelphia was the leading medical center of the Western Hemisphere, but the city's physicians were far too busy to be present for so commonplace an occurrence as a birth. The baby was named Payne.

Motherhood was a new and refreshing experience, incomparably exciting, and the 22-year-old Dolly lavished affection on her son. In her eyes he was perfect, an opinion to which she clung for many years, and in the long run she succeeded in spoiling him so badly that she caused herself grave problems. Her blindness to faults in him that others found obvious was one of her most glaring weaknesses.

"There is no other infant like him in all the world," she told Elizabeth Collins, who had been the attendant at her wedding.

If her intimate friend held a contrary opinion, she wisely kept it to herself.

Even though Dolly was preoccupied, she appreciated the honor when President and Mrs. Washington called on her. Her sister Lucy had married their favorite nephew, George Steptoe Washington, and had gone off to live with him at the Samuel Washington estate in Jefferson County, Virginia. So the President and First Lady were paying a family visit when they went to see Dolly.

Neither then nor at any other time was Dolly in awe of them. Like everyone else she called Washington "Your Excellency," which was the form of address used by virtually all of his subordinates, including those who had been associated with him for many years. The only known exception was Secretary of War Henry Knox, the one-time Boston bookseller who had become the commander of American artillery during the Revolution. Knox found it impossible to break his old habit of calling his superior General.

To Dolly, then and later, Mrs. Washington was "Aunt Martha." She was not yet acquainted with Mrs. John Adams, but the time would come when she would call the wife of the second President "Aunt Abigail." Her ease with the great and near-great, when she herself became the First Lady of the United States, is best understood perhaps when it is realized she had long been on familiar terms with the Founding Fathers and their families, and had been close to a number of them since childhood.

Settling into the routines of a Quaker housewife, Dolly took care of her baby, supervised the management of her home, and did most of the cooking. She saw her family often, and when her second sister, Anna, came home for holidays, the girl spent much of her time at the Todd house. Dolly's husband was devoted to her, and she dutifully accompanied him on twice-weekly visits to his own parents, who also lived in Philadelphia. According to the records of the Friends Meeting House on Pine Street, the young couple were faithful in their attendance there.

Busy in her own world, Dolly paid little attention to the formation and subsequent struggles of the new federal government. She saw Jefferson now and then when she went to her parents' home, and he duly admired her baby—having no choice in the matter—but it is impossible to imagine the Secretary discussing affairs of state with a girl the age of his own daughters. The lies that would be spread about Jefferson and Dolly a decade later, during his first term as President, referred to their alleged intimacy during this period, and were totally lacking in foundation. Nothing would have impelled the high-principled Jefferson to seduce the daughter of old friends—and under their own roof at that. And the young Quaker wife and mother was a woman of an integrity equal to his.

Dolly was busy in 1791, but her concerns were exclusively domestic. She had few household appliances, but food cost little, and her day-to-day existence was similar to that of countless women through the ages, none of whom ever achieved prominence.

Her father's condition continued to deteriorate. His physicians prescribed various medications, but none helped. On February 3, 1792, he slipped into a coma from which he never regained consciousness, and died seventy-two hours later. Walter came from Richmond for the funeral, as did William, who was living in New York, and Lucy Payne Washington hurried home from Virginia.

No one grieved more for John Payne than did Dolly and Anna, and the intimacy of the sisters seems to date from this time. Dolly was twenty-three and Anna was still in her midteens, but the difference in their ages was no barrier, and they remained close for the rest of their lives. Of all Dolly's sisters, Anna most resembled her in both appearance and personality. Exceptionally pretty, with the same coloring, Anna was plump and vivaciously extroverted. Years later, when she spent a great deal of time at the President's house in the new capital, Washington City, strangers sometimes mistook her for her older sister.

In the autumn of 1792 Dolly became pregnant again,

and on July 4, 1793, Independence Day, her second son was born. He was named William, after both her brother and John Todd's favorite uncle.

But the young mother had little opportunity to rejoice as she had when Payne came into the world. Within days of the baby's birth Philadelphia realized it was in the grip of a severe epidemic of yellow fever. The catastrophe grew, and would not end until the heavy frosts came in November.

The Congress had adjourned for the summer, but members of the executive branch had remained in Philadelphia, and they were becoming increasingly uneasy. The plague had no favorites, striking indiscriminately at men, women, and children of every class. The city's distinguished physicians tried every known remedy and in their desperation developed new methods of warding off the disease, but none were effective and no cure was known. Another century would pass before men would learn that yellow fever was carried by the mosquito *Aedes aegypti*.

Dolly was ordered by her husband and her physician to stay at home, venture out of doors only when necessary, and protect her babies. She followed the directions with care, and stopped to see her mother only long enough to assure herself that others in the family had not succumbed.

A letter written by Secretary Jefferson on September 8, 1793, to Congressman Madison, then in Virginia, indicates the gravity of the epidemic:

The yellow fever increases. The week before last about 3 a day died. This last week about 11 a day have died, consequently, from known data about 33 a day are taken, and there are about 33 patients under it. They are much scattered through the town, and it is the opinion of the physicians that there is no possibility of stopping it. They agree that it is a nondescript disease, and no two agree in any one part of their process of cure. The President goes off the day after tomorrow, as he had always intended. Knox then takes flight. Hamilton is ill of the fever, as is said. He had two physicians out at his house the night before last. His family think him in danger, & he puts himself so by his excessive alarm. He had been miserable several days before from a firm persuasion he should catch it. A man as timid as he is on the water, as timid on horseback, as timid in sickness, would be a phenomenon if his courage of which he has the reputation in military occasions were genuine. His friends, who have not seen him, suspect it is only an autumnal fever he has.

I would really go away, because I think there is rational danger, but that I had announced that I should not go till the beginning of October, & I do not like to exhibit the appearance of panic. Besides that I think there might be serious ills proceed from there being not a single member of the administration in place.

Government officials were not alone in fleeing Philadelphia. As the panic mounted, there was a general exodus, people of every class hurrying off to visit friends and relatives, or renting temporary quarters at country inns. The poor sometimes slept in the open fields, offering their services to farmers in return for food.

In many instances those who left Philadelphia were stricken elsewhere. Dolly, who was convinced there was no escape from the epidemic anywhere in Pennsylvania, was determined to remain in the city, and John Todd was reluctant to send her and the children away against their wishes. Then his parents came down with yellow fever, and the family's situation changed. He had to stay in Philadelphia in order to nurse them, and he insisted that Dolly and their sons go away.

She had no choice in the matter. With their faces wrapped in silk scarves, she and the children were bundled into a closed carriage and driven off to the village of Gray's Ferry on the Schuylkill River, where some cousins of the Todd family took them in.

Todd's parents died, but he remained in Philadelphia as a volunteer worker, believing his services were needed and convinced that he had developed an immunity to the disease. He worked until total exhaustion compelled him to join his family in Gray's Ferry. He arrived in mid-October, and a day or two later came down with yellow fever.

Dolly devoted her whole time and attention to him, staying at his bedside around the clock for the next three days. Suddenly she collapsed, and the one physician in the area diagnosed her ailment as yellow fever.

Her fever was so high that she became delirious, and although she did not know it, the physician felt certain she would die. But her constitution was strong, her will to live was unquenchable, and on October 22 she came to her senses after passing the crisis.

Not until she rallied was she told the stunning news that her husband and their infant son William had died of the disease. At the age of twenty-five she was a widow, and she had lost her baby, too.

The double tragedy slowed her recuperation, and it was December before she returned to Philadelphia with two-year-old Payne Todd. Members of her family expected her to move back to her mother's house, but she insisted on returning to her own home. She visited her mother frequently, but her actions made it clear that she intended to be her own mistress.

The estate left her by Todd made it possible for her to take an independent stand. She became the sole owner of the house on Chestnut Street, and Todd's cash bequest to her of $10,000 was the equivalent of $150,000 two centuries later. Dolly was not wealthy, but she was comfortably situated and beholden to no one. Unlike so many widows, she was not reduced to genteel poverty, and there was no need for her to marry in order to survive.

Her loss made it necessary for her mother to change her own plans. Mrs. Payne and her youngest children had been invited to make their home with her second daughter, Lucy Washington, in Virginia, but she postponed her departure until spring so she could remain near Dolly.

A steady stream of visitors called on the Widow Todd to pay their condolences, and one of the first was Martha Washington, who was accompanied by her young granddaughter, Nellie Custis. The First Lady emphasized that her own home, a nearby house rented from Robert Morris, was always open to the bereaved girl, and that she expected Dolly to visit her frequently.

Taking her at her word, Dolly often went to the Washington house. On her first visit, according to a letter she wrote to Lucy, she encountered the President, who asked what he might do to help ease her distress. "I told him," Dolly said, "that his friendship supported me." Even in a time of deep mourning her instinct prompted her to make a gracious reply.

The highest-ranking government officials were among the many who paid their condolences to the young widow. Secretary of State Jefferson and Attorney General Edmund Randolph, both of them lifelong family friends, came together, and were followed by Secretary of War Knox and John Jay of New York, Chief Justice of the Supreme Court.

Vice President John Adams returned to Philadelphia from Boston for the new session of Congress, and he was accompanied by his wife when he visited the Chestnut Street house. Dolly's friendship with the forthright Abigail Adams appears to date from this time, Mrs. Adams writing that she was "much impressed with the great & gallant spirit" shown by the younger woman. Courage in adversity, a most worthwhile character trait, was highly admired in the Adams family.

In the early years of the Republic the wives of most government officials stood apart from their husbands politically and took care never to set foot in that controversial arena. Hence it was possible for Abigail Adams to remain on cordial terms with Dolly even after she married James Madison, a confirmed Jeffersonian whose views on many matters of policy were opposed to those of John Adams. To an extent, perhaps, everyone involved realized that men who held high office were motivated by a deep, genuine desire to be of service to the young nation. In addition, their wives were members of a private "club," which forced them to endure many inconveniences and occasional hardships while enjoying few privileges.

Housing was short in Philadelphia, and the situation would be even worse in Washington City, which meant that, in the main, wives remained at home and spent the better part of each year without the company of their husbands. Government salaries were low, and those who lacked independent means struggled to make ends meet. So the wives of Presidents and Cabinet members, Congressmen and Supreme Court Justices understood the predicament of their sisters. All were in the same boat, and their mutual sympathies made it possible for them to ignore party lines in their own friendships.

The Congress reconvened in January, 1794, and soon thereafter James Madison paid a call on the Widow Todd. Only his signature in the guest book kept in the entrance hall indicates that he paid such a visit. Since he was a gentleman, correct in all things, it must be presumed that he remained for no more than the prescribed quarter of an hour and spoke of matters other than Dolly's bereavement.

Her period of official mourning, established by custom at three months in an era when life was short and perilous, soon would end, and a new phase of life would open to her.

VI

$\mathcal{S}$enator Aaron Burr of New York was a talented, hedonistic scoundrel, a man as ruthless as he was ambitious. A brilliant attorney and a clever politician, he stood out in an age of great men, but in 1794 his deviousness had not yet been revealed to his compatriots. Beyond all else he was a ladies' man, and in late February, when Dolly Todd put aside her widow's weeds, he took immediate notice of her. He was so charming, it was said over the period of his long life, that no woman could resist him, but Dolly was the exception.

When Burr, following the custom of the time, asked for the right to call on her, Dolly refused, offering no explanation. None was necessary. As she well knew, he was married to a woman ten years his senior, whom he had left behind on his handsome Westchester County estate. Under no circumstances would she become involved with him.

No one has ever discovered what sparked the interest of Representative James Madison in Dolly, but it is possible their paths crossed in her mother's house after her period of mourning, when he was calling on Secretary Jefferson. There was no more unlikely suitor for her hand. Forty-three years of age and seventeen years her senior, the Father of the Constitution was a confirmed bachelor whose friends had grown weary of trying to push him toward the altar. Everyone assumed he would never marry, and many Philadelphia mothers thought it a waste of time to present him to their daughters.

Madison had been so discreet in his private life that no hint of scandal had ever touched his name. His manner was precise, and although he displayed few idiosyncrasies, he had lived alone for so long that it was believed he was incapable of changing his habits. He dressed somberly, but with care, drank sparingly, and showed little interest in food. Ever since his student days at the College of New Jersey, later to be called Princeton, the creation of a strong, thriving United States had engrossed him, and he had devoted his genius to making that dream a reality.

Virtually everyone whose path crossed Madison's recognized his genius, and some were made uncomfortable by it. Others were kept at a distance by his dignified, rather cold manner. He rarely unbent in public, and even his speeches were formal, with a chilly undertone. His few close friends, among them Jefferson, several members of Virginia's Lee family, and, to a lesser extent at this time, James Monroe, knew he was genial, enjoyed and participated in conversations on many topics, and was not above exchanging gossip. Like all who had been reared on a plantation, he was an accomplished horseman, and he professed to like fishing, although he was inclined to let his mind wander into more important channels after he threw his hook and line into the water.

Apparently Dolly had no idea he was attracted to her, and she was startled when, a few days before her mother's departure for Lucy's Virginia home in April, 1794, she received a formal note. Mr. Madison requested the honor and rare privilege of calling upon Mrs. Todd the following Tuesday evening at eight o'clock. She had never thought of him as a suitor, but the note clearly signaled his intentions, and her mind whirled. Since she had never regarded him as a possible husband, she was uncertain whether to receive him. Even if she accepted, there was no time to have a new gown made.

Mary Payne, who was busy packing for her own journey, offered no advice when Dolly came to her for help. Surely a woman on the threshold of her twenty-sixth birthday, who had been married several years and had brought two children into the world, ought to know her own mind.

Dolly's spirit of adventure was so pronounced she could not refuse the request. In a hastily scribbled note to Elizabeth Collins Lee, her good friend, she indicated her willingness to suspend judgment until she looked at Mr. Madison in a new light, and she asked Mrs. Lee to attend her as a chaperone. Elizabeth, who admired Madison, sniffed the scent of romance in the air and happily assented.

The silver and pewter ornaments were polished, the furniture of oak and mahogany and maple was rubbed with the skins of citrus fruits imported from the West Indian Islands, and the hardwood floors were scrubbed. French tapers were exorbitantly expensive now that France was enmeshed in the throes of her own revolution, but a dozen were lighted in a gesture of careless extravagance.

Dolly wore a mulberry-colored gown, carried a tulle kerchief that matched it and, after changing her mind several times, tied a thin cap of off-white over her head. Curtsying to the floor when Madison bowed low at the parlor entrance, she noted he was dressed in a "black suit of seemly cut, a white shirt and black stockings of silk, with buckles of silver upon his shoes." No one appears to have paid any attention to the attire of the chaperone.

They discussed the Philadelphia weather, the poor

quality of silk currently being imported from France, their mutual hatred of the institution of slavery, kitchen gardens in Virginia, and the most effective methods of training house dogs. Whenever the conversation languished, Madison produced another subject. He was well informed but refrained from showing off his intellect, and Dolly was surprised by his quick wit. No matter who was speaking at any given moment, he kept his eyes on Dolly all evening, which made her slightly uneasy, and before departing he asked her to ride out into the country with him a few days later, bringing her small son with her if she wished. She realized he was pushing, but agreed.

That was the beginning. Always courteous, never exceeding the invisible boundaries of decorum and taste, Madison was unrelenting in pressing his suit. After a long life as a bachelor, he had fallen in love, and hating any kind of defeat, which he regarded as weakness, he was determined to win her. At first he saw her two or three times each week, but before long he was calling daily, sometimes stopping off for brief periods with a book for Dolly or a toy for Payne. He was distressingly blunt, making it plain that marriage was his object.

Never before had Dolly been subjected to such an overwhelming campaign, and she was confused. Young ladies didn't marry for love, which was a forbidden subject in patrician circles, and she was literally incapable of analyzing her own feelings. Unprepared for the onslaught, she resisted it.

Madison redoubled the fury of his siege and asked his heavy artillery for help. One day, when she was visiting Mrs. Washington, the President unexpectedly joined the ladies, of whom five or six were present. Suddenly tiring of their small talk, he launched into an impromptu speech in which he lauded the virtues of James Madison. No one in America had greater integrity or honor, no man was more gentle and considerate, he said. Someday, Washington predicted, Madison would become President, and then the whole world would recognize his worth. Someday he would marry, and his wife would be the most fortunate woman on earth.

A scarlet Dolly stared at the floor, enable to meet the President's direct gaze, and not until the following year was she able to joke about the occasion, thereafter referring to the remarks as "the President's Private Address to Mistress Todd."

Martha Washington was more circumspect than her husband and discussed Madison only when she and Dolly were alone, but her remarks were equally direct. Of all the bachelors she knew, she declared, Madison would make the best husband, and she added, "The esteem and friendship existing between Mr. Madison and my husband is very great, and we would wish thee to be happy."

Thomas Jefferson proved himself an accurate marksman when he fired his own salvos. He had watched Dolly grow to womanhood and had grieved for her in her time of sorrow. He had seen her at her best and worst, and as the father of daughters of his own, he presumed to believe he could read her heart. She would achieve her greatest contentment in life, he was convinced, if she married Madison.

Dolly wavered, almost gave in, and then drew back. Her sister Anna, recently returned to Philadelphia for a visit, was half in love with Madison herself, and urged Dolly to marry him. For years thereafter Dolly accused Anna and Madison of conniving, and they never denied the charge.

A change of scene might be helpful, Dolly decided, and she made up her mind to accept a standing invitation to visit Lucy Washington. Summer might not be the best time of year to go to Virginia, where the heat was even more intense than it was in Philadelphia, but no matter. She needed the opportunity to work through the problem on her own.

Madison, who had been successful in his efforts to win the adoption of the Constitution he had sired and who refused to admit the defeat of any bill he sponsored in the House of Representatives, had no intention of permitting Dolly to escape. Quickly agreeing when she told him of her plan to visit Harewood, the Samuel Washington estate, he proceeded to make all of the necessary arrangements for her.

He rented a carriage large enough for her, Anna, and little Payne, as well as their belongings. He interviewed a number of coachmen, and was not satisfied until he found one he regarded as reliable. He planned the itinerary, then wrote to several inns for advance reservations. He bought gift after gift for all three travelers to help them pass the time on the tedious journey.

Dolly planned to leave on July 1, and by an astonishingly curious coincidence the Congress adjourned for the summer on June 30. Blandly swearing that it would have been impossible for him to accomplish such a feat, a beaming Madison appeared on horseback the next morning and announced that he would escort the party. He said he was intending to spend the summer at his own home, Montpelier, in Orange County, and since he had no reason to tarry in Philadelphia, he would protect Dolly, her son, and her young sister from the terrors of the road.

He stationed his horse on Dolly's side of the carriage, and it occurred to Dolly that it might be impossible for her to dismiss James Madison even if she wanted to be rid of him.

The journey lasted a full week, and accommodations "happened" to be awaiting Madison as well as the others at every inn. He ate breakfast with Dolly's party, provided the food and wine each day for a roadside picnic at noon, and dined with them every night. He took charge at fords and ferries, paid off bargemen, and kept the disreputable at a distance. When three-year-old Payne tired of riding in the carriage, Madison hoisted him onto the saddle of his gelding, and the child enjoyed himself so much that after the first few days he spent the better part of each day on horseback. Pointing out places of interest, setting the pace, and preventing untoward incidents, Madison made himself indispensable.

In Orange County he turned off the new road to make his way across open country to Montpelier, and Dolly, who would reach her own destination the following day, admitted the past week had been the most pleasant she had ever known.

At Harewood she found neither solitude nor a chance to put her problem aside. Lucy and her husband George had been primed, presumably by young Washington's uncle and aunt, and they sang Madison's praises. Anna announced daily that she would die of unhappiness if Madison didn't become her brother-in-law. Even little Payne seemed to be joining in the conspiracy, and he wept when Madison didn't appear to take him for a canter.

Mary Payne was still no help and hinted that she believed Dolly had actually made up her mind but didn't know it.

Madison maintained his pressure, writing several letters each week to the young woman he wanted so desperately to marry. A master of concise clarity, a man whose prose works would be studied and appreciated for the next two centuries, Madison wrote impossibly clumsy love letters. He told Dolly in stilted phrases about his mundane activities at Montpelier, assured her of his undying love for her, and urged her to marry him without delay. His letters were formal, correct, and a trifle pompous; they were dull, totally lacking in the warmth he could reveal to Dolly in person. Apparently he expected few replies and was not discouraged, continuing to write even though he received only an occasional innocuous note from her.

Dolly was still uncertain whether she loved him, but by late August she could hold off no longer and gave in. Her sister and brother-in-law extended a cordial invitation to Congressman Madison to visit Harewood.

He arrived forty-eight hours later, so confident of success that he brought Dolly a heart-shaped gold locket that had belonged to his grandmother. She wore it until the end of her life.

The wedding took place on September 15, 1794, at Harewood, and was a gala event, with members of both families in attendance. Madison's brother was his best man, Lucy Washington was her sister's matron of honor, and the three younger Payne girls were among the bridesmaids, as was Madison's sister Fanny.

Dolly wore a gown of silvery satin, and afterward Madison distributed the lace ruffles from his shirt front to members of the wedding party as souvenirs. The bride seemed uneasy, and the bridegroom, as always in public, was somber.

But no effort or expense was spared to make the occasion memorable. Six fiddlers provided the music for dancing, and so many dishes were served at the wedding feast that they covered six large tables.

A shower of rice saw the bridal couple off on their honeymoon, which lasted a full month and which they spent at houses lent to them by friends in various parts of Virginia.

In mid-October James and Dolly Madison arrived in Philadelphia in time for the new session of the Congress, and everyone who saw them agreed that the bride was radiant and the groom less formal than he had been. The Washingtons, Jefferson, and all of Madison's other advocates had been right: Dolly had fallen in love for the first and last time in her life.

The intimacies shared by a couple were never a subject for discussion in eighteenth-century correspondence, but in the case of the Madisons it was unnecessary for friends to hint. The lifelong bachelor was giving his wife full satisfaction, which she returned in equal measure. The newlyweds seemed to be living in a blissful world of their own, and their friends and relatives, as well as Madison's colleagues, knew it.

The couple did not realize it, but they were making history. Even if Madison had not become President, even if Dolly had not developed into the most prominent of all American hostesses, posterity would have remembered their marriage as the happiest and most successful of love matches.

VII

*W*hen Dolly and James Madison returned to Philadelphia in mid-October, 1794, in time for the new session of Congress, they brought with them little Payne Todd, who was already calling Madison "Papa." Soon Anna Payne would join them and make her home with them, too. They took up temporary residence in the dwelling that had belonged to Dolly's first husband.

House hunting was the first item on Dolly's agenda, and she rented the place occupied the previous year by James and Elizabeth Monroe, who had told her it was now vacant. Space was at a premium in Philadelphia, and Madison urged his bride not to sell her house, but to use it as a steady source of revenue by renting it to others. She followed his advice, but was slow in buying the insurance policy on the place that he also suggested. Ten years would pass before she finally took the necessary action, and during that time Madison nagged at her frequently. As Dolly was the first to admit, she had no head for business and financial transactions made her nervous. Besides, she had other matters on her mind.

Paramount among the Madisons in the autumn of 1794 was the abrupt termination of Dolly's lifelong membership in the Society of Friends. The eighteenth-century

Quakers were as rigid in their attitudes as were those of older religions, which they criticized as unyielding. Dolly had married outside the faith; as a consequence, she was expelled from the Society.

She was hurt, but at the same time relieved. For many years she had secretly resented the restrictions on her conduct decreed by the only religious group with which she had ever been affiliated, and she had been held in line by fear. A letter she wrote eleven years later to Anna was revealing. Ill in Philadelphia in 1805, she was visited by a number of friends, including several Quaker ladies who reprimanded her for abandoning the principles of the Society. She wrote:

This lecture made me recollect the times when our Society used to control me entirely and debar me from so many advantages and pleasures and although [now] so entirely [free] from their clutches, I really felt my ancient terror of them revive to disagreeable degree.

Obviously, therefore, her removal from the Society caused her no real distress. She stood on the threshold of a new life, bolstered by her love for Madison and his for her. They had already formed an intimate relationship that would grow increasingly close through the years. In the brilliant career that awaited him as Secretary of State, President of the United States, and adviser to his successors, Madison never ceased to lean on Dolly while at the same time protecting her.

From the beginning of their marriage, they were inseparable. Dolly made it her business to travel with her husband whenever possible, and she saw to it that it always was possible, even though most women of the period remained at home. Rough roads, inadequate inns, and inferior meals held no terrors for her. Madison's health was delicate, as she quickly realized, and she

(71)

supervised every aspect of his private life, making certain that he was appropriately dressed in any weather, ate food that agreed with him, and conserved his energy. He, in turn, nursed her when she was ill, and although he never neglected affairs of state, he was sometimes placed under a considerable added strain because of his devotion to her.

Dolly's presence at her husband's side added a new dimension to American politics. Today the presence of an American official's or candidate's wife at various functions is taken for granted, but there were no precedents when Dolly became Mrs. James Madison.

Martha Washington, the first woman to become First Lady, acted as hostess at official dinners and receptions, but otherwise remained out of the limelight. Abigail Adams, retiring in her private life, felt it was wrong for a woman to take a prominent place in society simply because her husband was President or Vice President. And Jefferson was a widower.

So it was Dolly who became the pacemaker for all who followed her. She accompanied her husband on his campaigns. She cut ribbons, dedicated public structures, accepted trophies and gifts on behalf of the people, and even learned to deliver what was known, in an age of innocence, as a "patriotic address." Her speeches appear to have been somewhat less than immortal, none of them having survived.

Even more important than the other functions she performed, she became her husband's confidante. Madison trusted her completely, and proved it by discussing the details of his various involvements with her. While it would be absurd to claim that she was responsible for any of the major policies he developed either as Secretary of State or President, it is impossible to gauge the influence she may have exerted behind the scenes. She was so absorbed in him that his interests were her interests, and his love for her was so great that he was bound to listen to any opinions she may have expressed to him in private.

In one realm, certainly, her influence was great. Although she dutifully acted as hostess for all those whom she was required to entertain, her friendships often were responsible for the degree of intimacy Madison developed in his relations with others.

They were of one mind in their dealings with the Washingtons. The first President admired and respected Madison, also making it clear he liked Dolly. Both reciprocated his affection, and both were fond of Martha Washington.

Dolly and Abigail Adams, although dissimilar in every way, recognized a basic integrity in each other and consequently became friendly. Madison and Mr. Adams saw little of each other, perhaps because neither the policies nor the personality of John Adams appealed to him. Dolly might have built a bridge between the two men, but she, too, regarded Adams as cold and remote, and found she had little in common with him.

Nothing could have been more satisfying to Dolly and Madison than their close, mutual friendship with Jefferson. The two men long had admired and trusted each other, and by the time Madison married, he was already regarded throughout the United States as Jefferson's closest colleague and lieutenant. Dolly thought of Jefferson almost as a member of the family, after knowing him all her life and, in recent years, seeing him as a boarder in her mother's home.

Jefferson made no secret of his delight in their marriage, telling them and others that he knew no couple better suited to each other. He dined frequently at their home in Philadelphia, and when they were all in Virginia they often exchanged visits, with the Madisons going to Monticello and Jefferson riding to Montpelier. During Jefferson's Presidency he not only placed his trust in Dolly as his hostess, but enlisted her active help in his social battle with the British and Spanish envoys, a celebrated feud that will be discussed in a later chapter.

There can be little doubt that Dolly's relations with Elizabeth Monroe colored her husband's relations with James Monroe. The two men had been neighbors and friendly rivals in the earliest days of the Republic, and thereafter were closely associated. As Secretary of State, Madison was responsible for Monroe's appointment as minister to France. As President he gave Monroe the highest place in his Cabinet and virtually dictated the selection of the younger man as his successor. In spite of their professional closeness, however, the two men maintained a cool reserve in their personal relations.

The inability of their wives to attain more than a surface friendship was in large part responsible for the reserve. Dolly was beautiful, and Elizabeth was plain. Dolly was scintillating, and Elizabeth was retiring. Dolly was the acknowledged fashion leader of the Western world, but Elizabeth was dowdy, in spite of the years she had spent abroad. Dolly had a flair for putting others at their ease, while Elizabeth was so uncomfortable in company that others felt and reflected her distress.

It may be untrue that Elizabeth Monroe never resented the popularity of the more attractive woman, for she would have been more than human had she felt no jealousy. Both women were too discreet to air their opinions of each other, but their formality spoke for them. They exchanged courtesy calls when necessary, and both were studiously polite when they met at social functions. Elizabeth could not have been overjoyed when she discovered, after her husband became President, that many prominent Americans and foreigners still regarded Dolly as America's First Lady, and preferred to visit Montpelier to receiving an invitation to the President's house.

It is significant that Dolly and her husband held the

same views of others. She disliked Aaron Burr; so did he. She was unable to achieve a rapport with John Quincy Adams, and he was similarly afflicted. She developed a genuine affection for Andrew Jackson, the rough frontiersman, and Madison enjoyed his company, too. They saw little of Alexander Hamilton, but might have drawn closer to him, in spite of the widening political chasm that separated the two men, had Mrs. Hamilton spent more time in Philadelphia. Dolly met her only two or three times, but liked her, and wrote her a warm letter of sympathy after Hamilton was killed in his duel with Burr. The Edmund Randolphs were friends, and so were Cousin Patrick and Dorothea Henry, even though Governor Henry was becoming so cantankerous that it was difficult for anyone to get along with him.

Dolly became a social leader overnight after her marriage to Madison. Cast off by the Quakers, she could be herself at last, and her impact was immediate. Her charm entranced everyone, and her presence virtually guaranteed the success of a dinner party. Men besieged hostesses, clamoring for the privilege of escorting her to the table, and she was surrounded by admirers of both sexes at every function.

No longer required to wear drab clothes, she engaged a Mrs. Emory, who was much in demand as a dressmaker, to prepare her an entire new wardrobe of colorful gowns. Nelly Madison, her mother-in-law, gave her a number of necklaces, rings, and earrings that had been in the family for a long time, but she needed no jewelry to enhance her appearance, and formed the habit of wearing only one piece at a time.

Shoes were her greatest extravagance, and her husband indulged her whim by ordering twenty pairs of slippers for her from a Philadelphia bootmaker. She experimented with her hair, trying a variety of styles, but on most social occasions prior to the couple's temporary retirement to Virginia at the beginning of the Adams administration in 1797, she appeared with her hair piled high.

After their marriage the change in Madison's appearance became evident to everyone who knew him. Although he still wore suits of black or dark gray to sessions of the Congress, friends were pleased to see him in coats of brown, bottle green, and maroon that Dolly ordered for him from his tailor. His embroidered waistcoats were the envy of Aaron Burr, who thought of himself as the most elegantly attired man in government service, and most of Madison's shirts sported lace fronts and cuffs.

The difference in his attitudes was little short of amazing. For years he had rejected so many invitations that he had been regarded as a recluse, but now he went everywhere, his wife on his arm, and enjoyed himself thoroughly. At assemblies he proved himself an agile, graceful dancer, and at informal gatherings he unbent sufficiently to participate in parlor games.

But it was at dinners and receptions that he came into his own, thanks in large part to Dolly's adroitness. She realized that few conversationalists were his equal, and she wanted others to appreciate these talents, too. So she maneuvered him into groups where he would become the center of attention, cleverly making certain that someone whose interests were similar to his would make a remark that would spark him. By the time the couple left Philadelphia in February, 1797, Madison had acquired a reputation as America's most accomplished conversationalist since Benjamin Franklin had been in his prime.

James Madison had already achieved a permanent place for himself in American history by the time he married Dolly Payne Todd. His work in framing and winning the acceptance of the new Constitution had won him a niche as a Founding Father, so it is difficult to assess her contributions to his subsequent successes. Certainly she was influential in making him more approachable and in bringing out the warmth of his personality. Prominent men in government circles, who had once felt he was holding them at arm's length, now became friendlier with him.

While better social relationships neither won Madison his place as Jefferson's Secretary of State nor were directly responsible for his accession to the Presidency, people found they were able to deal with him more easily, and their willingness to work with and for him enabled him to govern more effectively.

From the beginning of his political career Madison had been in rapport with his Virginia constituents, and his platform manner had been surprisingly affable. After Dolly became his wife, she accompanied him on most of his political tours, and her presence in the front row of his audience was a distinct asset. In December, 1808, when Madison defeated Federalist Charles Cotesworth Pinckney of South Carolina for the Presidency by an Electoral College vote of 122 to 47, the unhappy Pinckney expressed the feelings of many when he observed, "I was beaten by Mr. and Mrs. Madison. I might have had a better chance had I faced Mr. Madison alone."

Too little was made by Dolly's early biographers of her ability to adapt to a new situation. When she married Madison in the early autumn of 1794, she had never danced, never held a playing card in her hand, and never attended a dinner party or reception, much less an assembly or ball. She learned so quickly that no one would have guessed she had entered a new world. The government had so few facilities of its own that most large affairs were held at Oeller's Tavern, the largest dining establishment in Philadelphia, and its top floor could be cleared for dancing. On one occasion, in the spring of 1795, President Washington announced as he

(77)

left the floor, "Mrs. Madison is the sprightliest partner I've ever had."

Dolly appeared to have an instinct for card playing, and Madison's analytical mind made him an expert at whist. The couple soon found themselves in demand, and within a year they were forced to give handicaps to couples with whom they played.

The first dinner Dolly attended was given by the Washingtons, a formal affair to which a number of foreign diplomats as well as American officials and their wives were invited. Wine was served with every course, and she took only a token sip, a practice she maintained for the rest of her life. Her own interest in cooking led her to pay particular attention to the many courses served by the proprietor of Oeller's, and within a few months she felt sufficiently confident of her own talents to begin giving a series of small dinner parties for Cabinet members, Senators, Supreme Court justices, and members of the House of Representatives. They won her overnight renown, and in 1796 Abigail Adams remarked that "an invitation to dine with Mrs. Madison is prized by all who are asked to her home."

Apparently Dolly needed no one to guide her through the social maze she had entered. She watched, listened, and then took action on her own initiative. Years later she was vastly amused when the Dutch minister, believing he was complimenting her, told her she was a superb hostess because she had never known any other life.

From the start of her new life Dolly retained an independent spirit, however, and refused to bow to the dictates of fashion for their own sake. Members of the American aristocracy long had been wearing wigs, and neither President nor Mrs. Washington ever appeared wigless in public.

Madison wore a wig in order to conceal his baldness, which grew more pronounced each year, and his wife approved. Just the same, she balked when he suggested that she wear one, too. Curiosity impelled her to summon a wigmaker to her house, and she tried on several models in front of a pier glass. But she dissolved in laughter, as did Anna, who recalled the event years later.

Most wigs then were powdered, and those who found them uncomfortable powdered their own hair, but Dolly also refused to accept the suggestion that she adopt that custom. She took pride in her hair, she said, and she refused to hide or transform it. She received so many compliments on her appearance that other ladies took note of the comments and decided to follow her example. By the time she left Philadelphia in 1797, only the old-fashioned were wearing wigs or powdering their hair, and ladies in Boston, New York, and Charleston were sufficiently emboldened to do as Dolly had done, too. For the first time she had influenced fashion.

There is no substance to the claim that Dolly was also the first woman in America to use cosmetics. Every lady carried a small container of rice powder and dusted her face with it to remove the sheen. Many used rouge on their lips and cheeks, but Dolly believed she had no need for the exorbitantly expensive substance, which was imported from France. On the other hand, she did emphasize her naturally long lashes by daubing them with a mixture of soot and grease, an early form of mascara. If she ever pasted a velvet beauty patch on her cheek, another widespread custom of the period, it did not appear in any of the many portraits of her that were painted over the years. Her own complexion was so attractive that it is unlikely she used more than token quantities of rice powder, which clogged pores and caused many ladies to look as though they were suffering from an acute attack of measles.

Dolly's delight in clothes was as great as her pleasure in discovering new recipes, and nothing better expresses her feelings than a letter she wrote in June, 1796, to Anna, who happened to be in Virginia at the time:

I went yesterday to see a doll, which has come from England, dressed to show us the fashions, and I saw besides a great quantity of millinery. Very long trains are worn, and they are festooned up with loops of bobbin, and small covered buttons, the same as the dress: you are not confined to any number of festoons, but put them according to your fancy, and you cannot conceive what a beautiful effect it has.

The hats are quite a different shape from what they used to be: they have no slope in the crown, scarce any rim, and are turned up at each side, and worn very much on the side of the head. The bonnets are all open on the top, through which the hair is passed, either up or down as you fancy, but latterly they wear it more up than down; it is quite out of fashion to frizz or curl the hair, and it is worn perfectly straight. Earrings, too, are very fashionable, and there is no such thing as long sleeves. They are worn halfway above the elbow, a black or a colored ribbon is pinned round the bare arm, between the elbow and the sleeve.

There have come some new-fashioned slippers for ladies, made of various colored kid or morocco, with small silver clasps sewed on; they are very handsome, and make the feet look remarkably small and neat.

While others hesitated after inspecting the new fashions, Dolly promptly ordered dresses, hats, and shoes made for her in the styles that suited her best. If the comments of her friends and the pride of her husband were accurate criteria, her taste was flawless. But she was always sensible. "I care not for newness, for its own sake," she wrote Anna. "I take and use only that which is pleasing to me."

VIII

*M*ontpelier, the home of the elder James Madison and his wife Nelly, was located about fifty miles northwest of Richmond, and the plantation's main house stood on the crest of a hill overlooking the Blue Ridge Mountains. It had been built almost a half century earlier, and was said to have been the first house in the county to boast a brick foundation. The couple's large family had been born and reared there, and the eldest son, James, who would inherit the property, felt a deep attachment to it.

Not until the Congress adjourned in March, 1795, did he have the opportunity to take Dolly home with him. Having met his parents, his brothers and sisters, and their families only at her wedding, she was justifiably apprehensive, but her husband soothed her verbally and in writing, assuring her that "they will love you as I do, beloved."

He was right. His father, in his seventies and in failing health, insisted that Dolly sit at his right every evening at dinner, and announced that he was little Payne Todd's grandfather. Nelly Madison and her new daughter-in-law achieved an even closer rapport; the older woman recognized the change for the better in her son and knew that Dolly was responsible. Within days of the couple's arrival at Montpelier, the women were exchanging confidences behind the closed doors of Nelly's sewing room, and Dolly learned for the first time that, during James's years at college, "never once did he commit an indiscreet act." He would have been a far happier young man, his mother said, had he erred occasionally, and she was lavish in her praise of the wife who had softened him.

Dolly and her mother-in-law became so intimate that, after the senior Madison's death, the old lady continued to live at Montpelier instead of accepting the invitations of her own daughters or other daughters-in-law to make her home with them. A new suite of four rooms was built for her convenience, and she spent many years in them, joining her son and Dolly when their company interested her, sometimes remaining in her own quarters when she was fatigued or wanted solitude. "We lived together in unbroken harmony," Dolly wrote many years later, "and never did an untoward word pass between us."

A large brood, now residing in various parts of Virginia, had lived on the extensive estate. One son, Francis, had died, leaving nine minor children, and another, Ambrose, would survive only a short time longer. His only daughter, Nelly Conway Madison, immediately became Dolly's favorite. Another brother, William, managed the estate in the absence of James. Two daughters and their husbands were visiting Montpelier: Nelly Hite and her husband Isaac; Sarah Macon and her husband Thomas. After the turn of the century a third daughter, Frances, would marry Robert Rose, a physician.

Frances, known in the family as Fanny, long had been close to her eldest brother, and at his insistence Dolly had corresponded with her since their marriage. But Fanny was unaffected by Dolly's charms, and Dr. Rose would share his wife's feelings. Madison had believed the two young women, who were approximately the same age, would become friends, but he was mistaken. Fanny, in person, was even cooler and more formal toward Dolly than she had been in her stilted letters.

Dolly took it for granted that people would respond to her in the same way if she liked them. She was somewhat bewildered by Fanny's attitude and wrote to Anna that she could only conclude that her sister-in-law wanted no woman to come between her and James.

Not until James Madison, Sr., died in 1801 did the real truth about the attitude of Dr. and Mrs. Rose become known. They were badly upset when Montpelier, which encompassed a tract of more than 5,000 acres, was left to the eldest son. They felt they should have shared in the bequest.

The Roses were the only members of the family who made trouble. Two mills were jointly owned by the heirs, and one was sold, with all sharing in the proceeds, while James acquired the other by giving various other properties in the county that he had inherited, 1,000 acres in all, to his brother and sisters. The Roses continued to protest, and since James wanted no dissension in the family, he voluntarily gave them grants of land elsewhere in Virginia and in Kentucky, as well as 550 acres of his primary inheritance in return for their mill shares.

Dolly made it her business to keep her opinions on the matter to herself. She stood aside during the negotiations with the Roses, neither interfering nor even hinting to her husband that she might regard them as greedy. It is significant, however, that Fanny and her busy brother drifted apart after his marriage, a process that became more rapid following the quiet dispute over their inheritance. At all times and under all circumstances Madison's behavior was that of the complete gentleman, so he never actually broke relations with Fanny, and was always courteous to her and her husband.

No criticism of Fanny, direct or implied, can be found in Dolly's correspondence, but her own natural dignity had been ruffled, and, consciously or otherwise, she never became close to Dr. and Mrs. Rose, for many years the relatives who lived closest to Montpelier. During the eight years Madison served as Secretary of State and the eight of his Presidency, his socially ambitious sister would have enjoyed sharing in his glory. But she and her husband were asked to attend only a very few functions at the President's House in Washington City, and there is no record indicating that they were invited to any affairs at Montpelier other than family get-togethers.

Amiable in her relations with almost everyone she encountered, Dolly was habitually quick to overlook slights and even insults directed at her. Margaret Bayard Smith, wife of the founder of the *National Intelligencer*, Washington's first daily newspaper, who moved to the new capital soon after the government was established there in 1800, was one of Dolly's greatest admirers, and in her *First Forty Years of Washington Society* indicated repeatedly that her idol, towering above her rivals, could afford to be generous toward them.

Dr. and Mrs. Rose were not treated with Dolly's usual generosity, however, and with good reason. Fanny had hurt and upset her brother, and when James Madison was disturbed, his wife leaped to his defense, giving no quarter. She could not or would not allow herself to forget that Fanny had wounded him.

When Dolly first visited Montpelier, the main house, thanks to several additions, consisted of twenty-nine rooms. She and her husband subsequently built a front portico, a terrace at the rear, and a new library, as well as Nelly Madison's four-room suite.

Dolly was reminded of Scotchtown and fell in love with the house that would be her new home. The central staircase gave the whole place an air of grandeur, the house boasted a dozen fireplaces, and even the kitchen outbuilding had stoves and hearths in three separate rooms.

Only the parlor was too formal for Dolly's tastes, and she later converted it into a cloakroom where visiting ladies could rest after suffering the rigors of the road. She moved the parlor to the old library, perhaps because its marble mantel was similar to that at Scotchtown. The library was her husband's private preserve, and there he read, studied, wrote, and conferred with visitors he elected to admit to the sanctum.

Other guests were not shown the library, even when being given the customary tour of the house, although it must have been the chamber they were particularly anxious to see. Only one servant was permitted to clean and dust there, and Dolly herself, totally unaccustomed to housework, accepted responsibility for straightening stacks of documents and emptying the wastepaper basket. Anything that added to her husband's comfort was her primary concern.

The gardens at the rear, which became her own preserve, appealed to her from the first, and she had the terrace built so she could sit outdoors and enjoy the view. The garden was divided into sections by trimmed hedges, a style adopted by many Virginia plantation owners, who were copying a design introduced by King Henry VIII's gardeners at Hampton Court Palace. Behind the beds of massed flowers, at the far end of the garden, was a maze, a set of connecting paths formed by double rows of hedges that stood seven feet high. Dolly promptly won the affection of her new nephews and nieces by playing hide-and-seek with them in the maze.

She also startled William Madison and her husband's sisters by running foot races with the girls of the family. Her parents-in-law were amused, and made it their business to cheer her, but Dolly's desire to be an athlete was greater than her talent for it, so she won few races.

Each morning she accompanied her husband on a ride through the fields, a practice they maintained for the rest of their lives when their health permitted. But Dolly returned to the house and joined her mother-in-law in the sewing room when Madison gave little Payne his daily riding lesson. She lacked his patience, she said, and the child responded more readily to instruction when she was not present.

While the senior Madison was still alive, he and his wife occupied some connecting rooms at the rear of the house, which they had used ever since the place had been built. The future President and his wife were given a suite on the second floor overlooking the front driveway, the most spacious suite in the establishment. It consisted of a large bedchamber, a sitting room, two dressing rooms, and even a private water closet, the only one in the house aside from that used by Madison's parents, which was not shared by family members and guests.

The bedroom walls were a pale green, while those of the sitting room were papered in gold and ivory stripes. There were draperies of dark green in both rooms, and most of the furniture, including an oversized four-poster bed with a feather mattress, had been made on the property. Dolly, who was delighted with the color scheme, proved herself a traditionalist by making only minor changes after she became the mistress of Montpelier.

Dolly and Madison spent six weeks at Montpelier, and by the time they returned to Philadelphia, the entire family, with the possible exception of Fanny and her husband, knew that the eldest son and heir had changed for the better as a result of his marriage. For the first time in his life he could relax, putting aside the problems of the nation and enjoying the pleasures that home life afforded him. Above all, his sense of humor had become more pronounced. His dry wit always had been a source of amusement, particularly at the dinner table, but now his jokes were broader, even when guests were present. Apparently he felt no need in private to draw into the somber shell that he maintained as a public posture until the end of his life.

One problem seemed insoluble. Both Dolly and Madison, like Jefferson, were incapable of reconciling principle and the reality of daily existence. Dolly had been opposed to slavery all of her life, and she never forgot that her father had freed his slaves when he had moved from Scotchtown to Pennsylvania. Madison and Jefferson based their opposition to the institution on intellectual grounds as well as the idealism that was always present as a motivating force in both men.

At the same time, however, the economy of their plantations depended on slavery. Further complicating the situation was Virginia law, which explicitly required slaves who were freed to leave the state permanently. This meant that men of conscience who emancipated their slaves felt compelled to assume the additional financial burden of establishing new homes and finding employment for the freedmen in the North. This might have been done in the case of house servants without too much difficulty, but it would have been impossible to place illiterate field hands, who knew no occupation other than the growing of tobacco and, to a lesser extent, cotton.

So Madison and Jefferson were reduced to opposing slavery in their written works while continuing to enjoy luxuries provided by the labor of their own slaves. It is going too far, perhaps, to claim they were ambivalent, and certainly they were not hypocritical. They were sincere in their belief, as Jefferson had first written in the Declaration of Independence, that all men were created equal and were equally entitled to life, liberty, and the pursuit of happiness. But they were victims of the social and economic structure of the society in which they lived. Only if Virginia had followed the example of Pennsylvania and other states of the North in abolishing slavery would it have been possible for them to free their own slaves.

Their alternative was bankruptcy and the loss of their homes. The government paid meager salaries, the Founding Fathers having adopted the British philosophy that service to the nation was an obligation accepted by men of means, and no man could have lived exclusively on what he earned in a government job. So Madison, Jefferson, and others like them in the South were trapped. They tried to change the system, but failed, and they believed that their only consolation was the hope that their efforts would lead to the abolition of slavery in the South.

In the meantime Madison and his wife treated their slaves with sympathy and compassion. They built substantial houses for the Montpelier field hands, were liberal in their grants of food and clothing, and made certain that adequate medical treatment was available. A number of visitors to Montpelier over a period of many years, among them the Marquis de Lafayette and General Andrew Jackson, noted in their correspondence that Dolly was particularly kind to her house servants, treating them with dignity and generosity. She and her husband did all they could within the limits of their own understanding to ameliorate the lot of those condemned to involuntary servitude, and nothing in their letters or other writings indicates any recognition of a possible inconsistency in their attitudes.

Their Philadelphia servants were free blacks, some of them former slaves whom Dolly's father had emancipated, and these members of their household were granted every possible consideration. Perhaps it is unnecessary to defend them, but at the least it is safe to assume they would have been shocked by the notion that some, in future generations, might regard them as two-faced.

IX

A French aristocrat named Moreau de Saint-Méry, who paid a long visit to the United States and was living in Philadelphia during the years immediately prior to the turn of the nineteenth century, was one of the few who failed to respond to Dolly Madison's charm or her husband's sober intellect. They were not alone in their inability to impress Moreau, who cordially disliked all barbaric Americans and their way of life. His comments on the Madisons are refreshing because they are the views of an outsider in no way awed by the accomplishments of the gentleman from Virginia.

Philadelphians, including the Madisons, he declared, considered their elm trees attractive, but he hated them because they sheltered countless mosquitoes. Drinking water had a metallic taste and was unpotable unless boiled. The brick sidewalks, which had gutters for drainage, were regarded by the Madisons as advanced, but actually were dangerous, thanks to the habits of Dolly and the city's other housewives. Every Wednesday and Saturday the sidewalks in front of each house were scrubbed. In summer the water failed to drain away because the gutters were choked with leaves, grass, and other debris; in winter the water froze and created a serious hazard for pedestrians.

Houses, including that which the Madisons had rented, were gloomy, hot beyond imagination in summer, and poorly ventilated in winter. Monroe had shipped his old friend large quantities of furniture from Paris, but Moreau still disapproved, saying that the style was tasteless and unimaginative. He also disliked American privies, complaining he was soaked by rain whenever he went to the toilet.

But the eating habits of Americans drew the worst of his ire, and it is obvious that Dolly was not yet serving many of the dishes for which she would become renowned. Moreau wrote:

They breakfast at nine o'clock on ham or salt fish, herring, coffee or tea, and slices of toasted or untoasted bread spread with butter. At about two o'clock they dine without soup. Their dinner consists of broth, with a main dish of an English roast surrounded by potatoes. Following that are boiled green peas, then baked or fried eggs, boiled or fried fish, the salad a thinly sliced cabbage, pastries, sweets to which they are excessively partial and which are insufficiently cooked. The entire meal is washed down with cider, weak or strong beer, then white wine. They keep drinking (Bordeaux or Madeira) right through dessert, toward the end of which any ladies who are at the dinner table leave the table and withdraw by themselves, leaving the men free to drink as much as they please, because the bottles then go the round continuously, each man pouring for himself. Toasts are drunk, cigars are lighted, diners run to the corners of the room hunting night tables and vases which will enable them to hold a greater amount of liquor. . . .

In the evening, round seven or eight o'clock (on such ordinary days as have not been set aside for formal

dinners) tea is served, but without meat. The whole fam-
ily is united at tea, to which friends, acquaintances and
even strangers are invited.

Moreau probably confused life under the Madisons'
roof with that of some of their less polished friends. They
often attended dinners similar to those he described, but
no one forgot his manners under Dolly's roof, and her
husband, who rarely consumed more than a single glass
of wine at a sitting, would have been the first to dis-
courage heavy drinking at his table.

John Adams dined at the Madison house that spring,
and was impressed by Dolly, writing to Abigail that she
was "a fine woman." He also praised Anna Payne, who,
in effect, had become the unofficial ward of the Madisons.

Girls in their midteens were eligible for courting, and
Anna was so popular that a steady stream of swains
called at the Madison house. Dolly's presence as a chaperone was mandatory, but she did not mind. She was so
high-spirited that she seems to have enjoyed these occasions, which made up perhaps for something that had
been missing from her own dour social life at the same
age.

The Philadelphia Quakers could not have approved of
any aspect of her busy existence. She and her husband
were in constant demand at festivals, balls, and dinners,
and she became an active member of the City Dancing
Assembly, the most prestigious social organization in Philadelphia. No party was complete without the presence
of Dolly Madison; gentlemen vied for the honor of escorting her to dinner, and members of both sexes crowded
around her in salons.

James Madison, having emerged from his own shell to
the extent that he was no longer painfully shy at a non-
political function, made no objection and enjoyed the stir
his wife created. He made no attempt to share the lime-

light with her, and preferred to confer quietly in a corner with other Congressmen, Senators, and Cabinet members.

In spite of Dolly's popularity, her conduct was circumspect, and she violated none of the mores of her time. Other wives sometimes flirted discreetly, but she held no brief for such behavior. As a consequence, the wives of those who sought her company knew their husbands' conversations with her were harmless. In an era when it was customary for a man's political foes to invent scandals about him and his family where none existed, not even the most rabid Federalist ever indicated in his private correspondence or otherwise that Dolly was anything but totally devoted to Madison. The unwarranted attempt several years later to couple her name with Jefferson's, as will be seen, was an effort to discredit the new President, and in no way reflected on Dolly's own high sense of morality, which was universally recognized.

One of the great disappointments of the married life of the Madisons was their inability to bring a child of their own into the world. When they were first married, they wanted children, but as the years passed they gradually abandoned hope. It would be wrong, however, to assume that this failure significantly changed their lives. No serious biographer of James Madison has claimed that the lack of a son and heir influenced his thinking. As for Dolly, she was a good mother to Payne and surrogate mother to Anna. But her husband came first.

James Madison felt the same way about her. In the early years of their marriage she had two sieges of serious illness, her symptoms indicating that she suffered attacks of malaria. Both times Madison immediately stopped all other activity to remain constantly at her bedside and nurse her back to health.

In 1796 Dolly began to emerge as a leader of American fashion. In March of that year the widow of a guillotined

French general, Josephine Beauharnais, was married to an even more prominent general, Napoleon Bonaparte, and almost overnight she influenced French styles. As daring in her attitudes toward clothes as she was reckless in her private life until Napoleon threatened to divorce her, Josephine favored clinging gowns and low necklines.

These styles quickly crossed the Atlantic, but they were regarded with uneasiness by most American women, who were still influenced by the heavy hand of colonial Puritanism. Dolly, however, was willing to accept a modified version of the new styles and had a gown made that was not quite as form fitting as Josephine's and which featured a not-quite-so-low neckline.

The dress was made of an imported gray satin, and again borrowing from Josephine, Dolly wore two sweeping plumes in her hair, securing them with a snug headband. She appeared in the costume at a ball given in October by the City Dancing Assembly and created a sensation. Madison was seen to smile proudly all evening.

A few ladies professed to be shocked, but the enthusiasm of their husbands for Dolly's appearance drowned their protests. The following day the dressmakers of Philadelphia were swamped with orders for similar gowns. Anna, who was caught up in the excitement, wrote at length to Lucy Washington and several of her own friends in Virginia about Dolly's triumph.

The girl's joy was short-lived. Naturally she wanted such a dress herself, but Dolly refused her request. It was fitting only for married women to wear such clothes. Those who were not yet protected by husbands, Dolly wrote Lucy, were "borrowing trouble," and the happily married Lucy smugly agreed. Several years later Dolly would wear a similar gown when she sat for her portrait by Gilbert Stuart, the most renowned American portraitist of the age.

Abigail Adams, the living embodiment of most Puritan attitudes, did not launch a direct attack on Dolly for adopting the new style, but called such clothes "really an outrage upon all decency." Launching an attack on an unmarried lady for wearing such a gown, Mrs. Adams then wrote:

Most ladies wear their Cloaths too scant upon the body and too full upon the Bosom for my fancy. Not content with the show which nature bestows, they borrow from art, and litterally look like Nursing Mothers.

Lucy had paid a visit to the Madisons by this time and had appeared in the new style, and Abigail Adams could not refrain from at least including the Payne sisters in her observations:

Since Dolley Madison and her sisters adopted the new fashions and seemed in every way delighted with the French-influenced manners of Philadelphia society, we may assume ex-bachelor Madison enjoyed fully the "luxurient" feminine displays for which "the Republican Court" of the seventeen-nineties was famous—or infamous.

Madison's marriage made him so contented that he seriously thought of giving up politics and retiring permanently with his wife to his family's Virginia estate. This resolve was strengthened by the election held in the autumn of 1796, when John Adams defeated Thomas Jefferson for the Presidency by an electoral vote of 71 to 68. Under the system then in effect, Jefferson became Vice President.

He, more than any other man, was aware of the contributions Madison had already made to the United States. He also recognized Madison's future potential worth to the nation. Alarmed by Madison's refusal to seek reelection to the House of Representatives or otherwise serve in the new administration, Jefferson wrote a firm letter. "Hold on then, my dear friend," he said. "I do not see a greater affliction than the fear of your retirement, but this must not be, unless to a more splendid and efficacious post." By this, it has been assumed, he referred to the Presidency, it having already become apparent to him that Madison was of the caliber to hold that office. He concluded, "Pray Mrs. Madison to keep you where you are for her own satisfaction, and the public good."

Governor Henry Lee of Virginia, with whom Madison had attended college, viewed the pending retirement of his friend with equanimity, perhaps because he was breaking with Jeffersonian doctrine and was inclining toward the views of Adams and the Federalists. Marriage, he wrote, was "softening" some of Madison's political "asperities."

As far as is known, Dolly did not influence her husband's desire to retire from the political arena. She thoroughly enjoyed the hectic life they were living in Philadelphia and, like all Americans, was looking forward to the creation of the nation's new capital, Washington City, on the banks of the Potomac River. At the same time she was prepared to settle down as a planter's wife in rural Virginia. It would not have been seemly for a wife to interfere, and the Madisons, no matter how deeply they loved each other, observed the proprieties of their era. It is likely, too, that by now Dolly knew her strong-willed husband sufficiently well to realize he would make up his own mind in his own way. Her role was to contribute to his happiness and stability, and this she did.

There is no hint in the correspondence of either that Dolly influenced his decision to retire or that she regretted it. Madison, to be sure, rarely mentioned his wife in his correspondence with others. As much as he may have relished her social triumphs, he did not regard her activities as an appropriate subject of discussion with the outside world.

It would be a mistake to emphasize too strongly the possible effect of Madison's marriage on his retirement. He had given thought to the matter prior to marrying Dolly, in part because of his growing dislike of Hamilton and the Federalists. There can be little doubt, however, that his personal happiness spurred him to a more active consideration of his urge to leave the political arena.

When the Madisons left Philadelphia, almost on the eve of John Adams' inauguration as President, they had every expectation of spending the rest of their lives at Montpelier. What they failed to take into account was that James Madison was in the prime of life, and when he saw the Federalists increasing the powers of the national government at the expense of the states, he became alarmed. He held, with Jefferson, that all powers not specifically delegated to the federal government were reserved by the states, and his sponsorship of this position was one of the major factors that would drive him back into politics.

He was worried, too, by the sharp decline in Franco-American relations, which led to an undeclared war between the United States and her former ally during the latter years of Adams' Presidency. And he was also concerned about the new nation's increasing frictions with Great Britain. The United States would survive as an independent, free country only if she had the opportunity to develop her economic potential in a time of peace. These concerns also played a major part of his continuing alliance with Jefferson.

All the same, he thought of himself only as a planter when he returned to Virginia, and Dolly had every reason to believe that her brief stay in the national limelight had ended. She apparently knew, however, that she would be active as a hostess at Montpelier, and had a number of new gowns made before leaving Philadelphia.

The house was far less crowded than when she had first visited it. The Hites were spending most of their time on their own estate, where Dolly and her husband had visited on their honeymoon, and most of the others had gone elsewhere, too.

So there was ample room for the heir to Montpelier and his wife, five-year-old Payne, and Anna, who was given a small sitting room of her own as well as a bedchamber. Nelly and the senior Madison were still mistress and master of the establishment, but ill health had made them weary, and they willingly granted the newcomers many of their responsibilities and prerogatives.

For the moment James Madison had nothing other than Montpelier to occupy his mind, and he took active charge of the estate, supervising the sale of tobacco, increasing the yield, and keeping the account books. He proved himself a competent businessman and within a year almost doubled the plantation's profits.

Dolly took over the operations of the household from her grateful mother-in-law and happily settled into an adult version of the life she had known at Scotchtown. She planned meals, ordered food supplies, and kept an eye on the kitchen garden. She supervised the cleaning and maintenance of the house, bought new furniture, and took charge of repairs. She directed the making of new clothes, sewing many garments herself, and made a daily tour of the property in order to ensure that the sick were attended.

It was a tribute to both Dolly and her mother-in-law that the combined family groups were able to live together with a minimum of friction. This they accomplished by occupying different sections of the house and going their separate ways wherever possible. They came together only for meals, and the senior Madisons, who were tired of social life, dined in their own quarters when Dolly and her husband entertained.

Nelly Madison maintained a lively interest in the gardens, but no longer worked in them. She was content to sit in the sun and watch as Dolly spent an hour or two each day weeding, pruning, and planting. The older woman approved of her daughter-in-law's efforts and refrained from expressing criticism on the infrequent occasions when she disapproved. Dolly was equally careful to defer to her, so their relations remained harmonious.

There were no cities of consequence in Virginia at the turn of the nineteenth century, so the state's aristocrats maintained the patterns of social life that had originated in colonial times. Relatives and friends visited each other incessantly, stopping only for dinner at the homes of near neighbors, but remaining overnight or longer elsewhere after spending hours on the road. It was not uncommon to travel from one house to another on peregrinations through a county, and guests were inclined to stay for several days after going from one end of the state to the other.

Dolly and her husband took an active part in these exchanges of visits, particularly during the winter months, when their presence was less urgently required at home. Their schedules were sometimes strenuous, and they were known to visit as many as five different estates in a single week.

Thomas Jefferson was a frequent guest at Montpelier, stopping there several times each year, and soon after the Madisons returned to Virginia from Philadelphia, they inaugurated the custom of paying at least two prolonged annual visits to the Jefferson estate, Monticello. No record was made of conversations on these occasions, but it is highly improbable that the two future Presidents of the United States talked only about crops and the weather.

Ladies were expected to show no interest in politics, but Dolly often was present, and in later years, when she and her husband were separated for brief periods, she demonstrated her grasp of state affairs by asking pertinent questions, in her letters, about both domestic and foreign matters.

In 1797, when James and Elizabeth Monroe returned home from Europe, they had built a new home only a short distance from Montpelier, and the two families frequently exchanged dinner visits. Monroe, who would succeed Madison as President, liked to stretch his long legs after a meal, so the two men went for protracted walks, leaving their wives behind to cope with each other as best they could.

Both were ladies, so they managed, usually confining their chats to domestic trivia. Their interests were more nearly alike than either realized, but Dolly's charm and beauty, combined with Elizabeth's feeling of insecurity, made it difficult for them to establish a real friendship. Their husbands' close political association over a period of many years forced them to spend many hours together, but they never became intimate and, as far as is known, never addressed each other by their Christian names. Even the few letters they exchanged were formal notes.

If their backgrounds were any criteria, Elizabeth Monroe should have been the more sophisticated. She had been born in New York, where she had been reared in a prominent, financially comfortable family, and she had enjoyed the benefits of living and traveling in Europe for an extended period. But she remained retiring, had little interest in clothes or food, and although she became a gracious hostess, she regarded entertaining as a chore. It would have been unthinkable for ladies of the period to discuss the business that occupied their husbands, so she and Dolly must have found it difficult to dredge up topics of conversation.

As Martin Van Buren, the eighth President of the United States, observed many years later, however, "Mrs. Madison's talk at dinner is free on any matter." Dolly didn't yet realize it, but she was already the compleat statesman-politician's compleat wife, able to get along with anyone into whose company she was thrown.

X

$\mathcal{A}$lthough James Madison believed he had abandoned politics when he took his family to Montpelier, the four years he and Dolly spent in full-time residence there strengthened his base of operations. Until his marriage he had returned home only for brief visits, spending most of his time in Philadelphia and New York. Now, however, other Virginians thought of the Madisons as real neighbors, and the combination of his intellect and his wife's hospitality won him widespread support. Men who had stood behind Washington of Mount Vernon were now swearing fealty to Jefferson of Monticello, Madison of Montpelier, and Monroe their neighbor, and the Virginia dynasty feared by the Federalists of New England and, to a lesser extent, the states of the New York–Pennsylvania axis was becoming a reality.

Montpelier was the rock upon which the Madisons founded their lives. They returned home whenever possible during their sixteen-year sojourn in Washington City, and aside from an occasional trip to Philadelphia, they went nowhere else. Travels within Virginia, of course, were not regarded as real journeys.

In 1798 Madison became the official guardian of the daughter of his late brother Ambrose and was required to act as the administrator of her property. Nelly, not yet in her teens, came to Montpelier to live. Madison was deeply involved in a dispute of the greatest importance to the United States, so Dolly accepted the major responsibility for the girl, acting as a foster mother and bringing her up as her own child.

Her husband neglected none of his duties at the plantation, but he was busier and more preoccupied than at any time since he had left the House of Representatives. He and Jefferson were outraged by the Alien and Sedition Acts, which had been pushed through a pro-Federalist Congress by the Adams Administration. They believed that the acts threatened the personal liberties of the American people and that the federal government had assumed unwarranted and unconstitutional powers that belonged to the states.

The two Virginians held a long strategy meeting at Montpelier and then went their separate ways, Jefferson to write a condemnation of the Alien and Sedition Acts that would be passed by the Kentucky legislature and Madison to do the same for the Virginia legislature. The results of their labors, the Virginia and Kentucky Resolutions, would become the philosophical keystones on which the future of the Republican-Democratic party would be built.

A question that has troubled a number of scholars, that of the extent to which Madison relied on the work of his friend and mentor, need be mentioned only in passing. The two men understood each other so well that they were of one mind, working independently of each other without the need to meet or correspond frequently.

Madison was convinced the Republic was in danger and acted accordingly. Dolly curbed their social life, accepting no invitations that would require their overnight absence from Montpelier and inviting fewer guests to dinner. She had to make certain, too, that Nelly and

Payne created no disturbances when Madison was pondering and writing in his study. These were her major contributions to the Virginia Resolution, and the claim of her enthusiastic mid-nineteenth-century biographers that she had a hand in its preparation is absurd. Madison needed no help from his wife in understanding the principles of democratic government, and whatever knowledge of the subject she may have acquired, if any, she learned from him.

Vice President Jefferson continued to draw his friend and protégé deeper into politics. By late 1798 the battle over the powers of the federal government was fully joined. President Adams found an exceptionally able advocate of his views in John Marshall of Virginia, and the future great Chief Justice of the United States Supreme Court wrote a powerful treatise upholding the Federalist position.

Hoping to counter its influence, Jefferson urged Madison to reply in a series of weekly articles or letters to the newspapers. The master of Montpelier realized he would be able to devote even less time to his family and the managment of the plantation, but felt obliged to accept. He closeted himself in his study daily, and Dolly permitted no one to interrupt him, curtailed their social life still more, and continued to keep the children quiet.

She was being forced into increased isolation, a life that was a far cry from the social whirl she had enjoyed in Philadelphia or the convivial round of activities she had first known in Virginia. But she never complained, not in her letters to her mother and Lucy Washington nor to anyone else. She accepted any life her husband chose for them; whatever he believed right and just became her cause, and she sought only his happiness.

In 1799 new complications again quickened the pace of life. Madison learned through Dolly's family that Cousin Patrick Henry was planning to return to politics after years of retirement and would run for the Virginia legislature in order to further the Federalist cause there. The news was alarming. The old Patriot still commanded a devoted following, and he was such an accomplished orator that it was possible he could carry Virginia into the Federalist camp.

Dolly confirmed the rumor in an exchange of letters with her mother, and Madison knew he had to take direct action to counter Henry's influence. He discussed the problem with Monroe, wrote to Jefferson, and soon thereafter went to Monticello, taking Dolly with him. As usual, they were quartered in their favorite room, which was always kept for their use and was now known as the "Madison chamber."

Jefferson heartily approved of his friend's plan: Madison intended to run for the legislature as a representative of Orange County, and if elected would rally the Republican-Democrats in opposition to Henry. Announcing his candidacy to neighbors as soon as he and Dolly returned home, Madison lost no time opening his campaign.

Politics was still regarded as an exclusively male concern, so eyebrows were raised when Dolly accompanied her husband to major rallies and sat in the front row when he delivered his speeches. Her own popularity in the county made it difficult for Madison's opponents to criticize her, and soon the wives of other candidates began to appear in public, too. Dolly had no idea she was setting a precedent for American political campaigns of the future, and it would not have occurred to her that she herself might influence any voters. Her motivation was neither wily nor subtle: she attended the rallies for the simple reason that she wanted to hear her husband speak.

But Dolly would do nothing to embarrass her husband or herself, so on some occasions she wisely remained at home. Drinking was heavy, language was rough, and men engaged in crude horseplay at political picnics and other outings, so ladies were conspicuous by their total absence.

Madison won his election with ease, and all Virginia looked forward to the confrontation of the "little giant" and the "old giant." The coming conflict was important beyond the state's borders, too, and newspapers elsewhere wrote at length about the pending political duel. But the fight never did take place because Patrick Henry died after a brief illness, before Madison could be seated.

James Madison went off to Richmond for the meeting of the House of Delegates, and although he sought no leadership, the Republican-Democrats willingly became his followers. A spell of fine weather promised a bumper crop throughout the state, so the meeting of the legislature was brief, the members wanting to return home in time for the harvest.

In December, 1799, the shocking news reached Montpelier that George Washington had died at his Mount Vernon estate. Dolly and Madison immediately canceled a small dinner party and left that same day for the funeral. Every prominent Virginian hurried to Mount Vernon, and scores came from other states, too, to pay their last respects to the great general and President.

Dolly, who was always in command of herself in the presence of others, was seen to weep in public for the first time. But she regained control of her emotions before expressing her condolences to Martha Washington. Her grief was so great, as was her husband's, that, according to a letter she wrote Lucy, "we exchanged scarce a word on our sad journey home."

Three weeks later James Madison returned to Richmond, this time to attend a meeting of Republican-Democrats from every part of the state. The air was filled with politics, and the master of Montpelier seemed to have forgotten that he had retired from the arena. The impending candidacy of Thomas Jefferson for the Presidency of the United States became his first concern.

At first glance the situation looked promising for Jefferson. He had struck a deal with Aaron Burr, who had agreed to run as the Republican-Democratic candidate for Vice President, and who appeared likely to sway many Federalist voters in New York, Pennsylvania, and portions of New England, particularly Rhode Island.

Equally important, the Federalists were in disarray. The nation had soured on President Adams, in part because of his sponsorship of the unpopular Alien and Sedition Acts and partly because of the undeclared Franco-American War. Even more important, John Adams lacked the ability to unbend in public, and his unintended pomposity made him many enemies. Politicians realized, too, that his split with Alexander Hamilton diminished his chances of winning the New York electoral vote.

But the Republican-Democrats were taking no unnecessary risks. Federalist John Marshall had been elected to the House of Representatives the previous year, the party's following in the state was strong, and Jefferson would be discredited if he failed to win an overwhelming victory in his home state.

Madison was determined to prevent such a catastrophe. In spite of his almost instinctive dislike of electioneering, he became the cool-headed professional when he descended into the pit. Others might enjoy the rough-and-tumble, but none could match his analytical acumen. His fellow Republican-Democrats turned to him for guidance at the week-long conference, both because of his intellectual prowess and because it was known by all that he was Jefferson's closest confidant and collaborator.

Madison voluntarily assumed a heavy role. He accepted nomination for the post of an elector, became chairman of the Orange County committee for the election of Jefferson, and agreed to serve on a five-man central, or coordinating, committee.

When he returned to Orange County, his days were filled with correspondence, and politicians came to Montpelier from every part of the state. Dolly was equally busy. Not only was she required to entertain the small army of political guests who poured through the house, but she had to supervise the building of the new portico and terrace, which were added that spring. A heavy snow fell early in February, the bitter cold was unremitting for six weeks, and Dolly assumed an additional burden, that of soothing her apprehensive husband, who was afraid the plantation's crops would be badly damaged. On top of all the other worries, Madison's seventy-six-year-old father displayed the first signs of the illness that would prove fatal the following year.

Jefferson stopped off at Montpelier, traveling to and from his own home, and the Madisons paid several visits to Monticello in the crucial spring and summer of 1800. Jefferson and Burr were opposed by President Adams and General Charles C. Pinckney of South Carolina, the most strongly Federalist of the Southern states. In most states the electors were chosen by the legislatures, and the results promised to be too close for comfort. Dolly and Jefferson's daughter Martha, who spent much of her time at Monticello, were inundated with politics, since Jefferson and Madison could discuss little else.

It was generally assumed that New England, with the exception of Rhode Island, would end in the Federalist camp, that the South and West would favor the Republican-Democrats, and that the balance of power lay in the mid-Atlantic states. But Madison predicted that surprises were in store for both parties.

In the late spring he was encouraged by news from New York. Hamilton's lack of enthusiasm for the Federalist ticket had enabled Burr to gain control of the legislature, and the state's vote for the Republican-Democratic ticket would be solid. But not until the beginning of November, when the new Congress convened for the first time in Washington City, did the situation begin to clarify.

As expected, most of New England was solidly Federalist. Burr's optimism about Rhode Island proved unwarranted, and she, too, ended in the Federalist column. Madison's efforts in Virginia resulted in a Republican-Democratic landslide there, and the party also triumphed in Georgia, Tennessee, and Kentucky. But the Federalists countered by winning in two unpredictable states, New Jersey and Delaware.

North Carolina and Maryland permitted split-ticket balloting, and the Federalists gained again, picking up 4 out of 12 votes in the former and 3 out of 8 in the latter. Only South Carolina and Pennsylvania had not yet voted, and their decision would be critical. Madison and Jefferson believed the Republican-Democratic candidates would win by a narrow national margin of 5 votes.

The Pennsylvania legislature was evenly split, the votes of one party neutralizing those of the other. Everything now depended on South Carolina, where the Republican-Democrats waged a bitter fight and finally emerged victorious in the legislature.

Those who believed Jefferson had won the Presidency celebrated prematurely. Adams and Pinckney were defeated, to be sure, but Jefferson and Burr, the supposed Vice Presidential candidate, each received 73 Electoral College votes. Under the Constitution the election would have to be decided by the House of Representatives. But election rules had not yet been clarified to the extent that two members of the same party would be prohibited from facing each other in a runoff.

Many members of both parties assumed that Burr would abide by what had been an informal gentlemen's agreement and would stand aside for Jefferson. But many who were well acquainted with Aaron Burr were not surprised when he proved to be no gentleman and refused to withdraw.

Whether Dolly Madison ever told her husband, either at this time or previously, that Burr had made delicate but definite improper advances to her when she had been a widow is unknown. If Madison had no personal reason for despising Burr, he loathed him on exclusively political grounds. Mincing no words, he charged that Burr had connived from the outset to win the election himself, and he repeated the indictment until the end of his life.

The Father of the Constitution was trapped by clauses in that document he had himself written, and his outrage was boundless. In the first weeks of 1801 he proposed a number of schemes, all of them both legal and ingenious, to win the election for Jefferson.

Meanwhile the issue remained in doubt, and not until mid-February, 1801, was it resolved by the abstention of several moderate Federalists. Thomas Jefferson was elected President, and Aaron Burr became Vice President.

No historian has been able to determine when Jefferson asked James Madison to take the top place in his Cabinet and serve as Secretary of State. But it was taken for granted from the time the Republican-Democrats met in Richmond in January, 1800, that Madison would be given a high office in a Jefferson Administration.

In all probability Madison himself made such an assumption, and so did his wife. He was convinced, no less than was Jefferson, that the very form of government established in the United States under the new Constitution was being subverted and destroyed by the Federalists, and that only the Republican-Democrats could preserve the independence of the Union whose territory was still coveted by the major powers of Europe.

An equally important consideration was the closeness of his personal ties to Jefferson, his most intimate friend as well as his political mentor. To have refused an appointment would have been an act of disloyalty to Thomas Jefferson the man, as well as to the nation both had been so influential in creating.

It is difficult to imagine that Dolly failed to share her husband's feelings. Aside from her overwhelming desire to stand by him in all things, to help and sustain him, she herself had forged a strong, firm friendship of her own with Jefferson. She could not remember a time in her life when she had not known him, and if she did not think of him as a substitute father, at the very least she regarded him as a favorite uncle. To have rejected his plea for assistance when he needed it, at a time he and Madison believed critical for the future of America, would have been to abandon her own sense of honor.

Whatever ambitions Madison may have entertained for himself and Dolly may have felt undoubtedly flared at this time, too. For years Jefferson had made it plain that his friend was of Presidential caliber. Ordinarily the Vice President would have been the heir apparent, particularly when he and the President were members of the same party, but Aaron Burr, regardless of whether he had indulged in chicanery, had alienated too many Republican-Democrats to be considered a potential candidate in 1804 or 1808. This meant the Secretary of State would become the crown prince, and no one knew it better than the analytical Madison.

Jefferson invited his friend to join him in Washington City in February, before the House of Representatives took its final vote, but the offer was declined. Always sensitive to public reactions, Madison did not want to be placed in the position of seeming to be an office seeker. Moreover, grave personal problems kept him at home throughout February.

Madison's father, now seventy-seven years old, was seriously ill, and his physicians confessed that they were powerless to preserve his life. The family began to gather at Montpelier, and the end was expected at any time. Madison was suffering from complications of his own, too. An attack of rheumatism sent him to his bed in the second week of February, and Dolly immediately prescribed the regimen of the period, swathing him in flannels and depriving him of wine and other alcoholic beverages, but his recovery was slow, and travel was inadvisable.

On February 28 James Madison the elder died, and several hundred prominent Orange County neighbors and friends attended his funeral. Dolly had to look after her mother-in-law as well as provide refreshments for the many callers who came to the estate, and her husband, who was his father's principal heir, retired to his study to confer with his siblings and a number of attorneys.

By this time he knew he would be named Secretary of State, but circumstances made it impossible for him to leave home in time for Jefferson's inauguration ceremonies on March 4.

XI

*T*he new capital of the United States, officially known as Federal City until its name was changed by a bill sponsored by the Jefferson administration, resembled a frontier boom town in the early months of 1801. John and Abigail Adams had lived for a few months in what they had called the President's Palace, but carpenters and painters were still putting finishing touches on the place. The headquarters of various government departments were completed, but work was still in progress on the Capitol, the carpenters being forbidden to make undue noise when the Congress was meeting.

Land speculators had purchased large tracts of property on which private houses were being built, but most of the buildings that were already occupied or almost ready for occupancy were boardinghouses. As yet the town had no taverns or other eating places, no hospitals, and no schools. Two general stores had opened their doors in January, and scores of other retail establishments were being constructed. There were no public meeting places other than the government buildings. Carpenters and masons worked day and night to make the foreign legations habitable. Parks existed only on paper, and the so-called roads were no more than rutted ribbons of dirt.

It was believed that within a few months construction plans would be sufficiently advanced to provide living space for a population of eight thousand. It was estimated that at least five thousand were already crowded into the town, with as many as eight men sharing a room.

Outgoing President Adams and his blunt wife did not wait until the end of his term to return to Massachusetts, and at the end of February they left the town that everyone had already taken to calling Washington City. Some of Adams' Cabinet members did the same, relieved to be ending their stay in the perpetually damp community on the Potomac. Many Federalists were loud in their criticism of the site, saying the chill was penetrating in winter and the heat unbearable in summer. The Republican-Democrats labeled these protests political, but a year later they were equally vocal.

At his boardinghouse President-elect Thomas Jefferson, thanks to the dignity of his coming high office, enjoyed the rare privilege of sleeping in a private bedroom. On the morning of March 4 he signaled the beginning of a new, unpretentious era by going on foot to the Capitol to take his oath of office and then marching through the mud of what was euphemistically called Pennsylvania Avenue to the Chief Executive's office-residence, which he promptly renamed the President's House. No members of his Administration had as yet arrived, hence none were on hand for the informal reception that marked the beginning of what Jefferson himself termed the "new revolution" in the United States.

The next morning members of the household staff recruited from Monticello served the usual early breakfast, and promptly at 8 A.M. the President announced his Cabinet appointments. No one was surprised to learn that

(113)

the group would be headed by Madison as Secretary of State. The Swiss-born Albert Gallatin of Pennsylvania and later New York, who had lived for a time on the frontier in western Pennsylvania and who had demonstrated as a member of the House of Representatives that he was something of a financial wizard, was made Secretary of the Treasury. Since he was a friend of Madison and a former colleague, it was certain that relations between State and Treasury, the two most important Departments, would be harmonious.

These two appointments gave the Federalist press the opportunity to make jokes at the expense of the new Administration. Jefferson, these newspapers said, was so anxious to outshine his own Cabinet that he chose two men whose combined height was less than his own. This was something of an exaggeration: the President was six feet, two and one-half inches tall; Madison stood at five feet, six inches, and so did Gallatin.

Levi Lincoln of Massachusetts became Attorney General; Major General Henry Dearborn of the same state, who was inept but enjoyed the trust of War of Independence veterans, was made Secretary of War; and Gideon Granger of Connecticut was appointed Postmaster General. Jefferson was still searching for a Secretary of the Navy. It was rumored that James Monroe might be offered the post, and Madison sounded him out on Jefferson's behalf. However, Monroe preferred, for the present, to continue to serve as governor of Virginia, a position to which he had been elected in 1799.

A scant week after his inaugural the President left Washington to pay a short visit to Monticello, and he followed his usual custom of stopping overnight at Montpelier. Dolly was not surprised to discover that the President of the United States, having already discarded the elegant coach of state pulled by six matched horses that Adams had acquired, was traveling alone and on horseback. Jefferson was sincere in his desire to rid his office of any trappings reminiscent of European royalty, and he lived accordingly.

According to a legend that cannot be verified or disproved, some part of the dinner-table conversation that evening was devoted to the minor problem of finding a new form of address for the nation's Chief Executive. Washington and Adams had been called "Your Excellency," but Jefferson thought the name too formal. By the time the meal ended it was decided that "Mr. President" was suitable, and the term has been used down to the present day. Whether Dolly was the originator of the phrase is debatable. Madison, Jefferson himself, or various members of the Madison family who were present at the table that night might have been responsible.

After dinner the President and the Secretary of State-designate retired to the study, where they conferred until early morning. Their principal problem, Madison told his wife when he finally joined her, was how to get rid of Federalists who held important government posts and appoint Republican-Democrats in their stead.

Jefferson returned to Washington City soon thereafter. Before he left, he was disturbed to find that Madison's rheumatism had taken a turn for the worse, forcing Dolly to confine him to bed. But the squire of Montpelier expressed his desire to take up his duties as quickly as possible, and swore he would come to the capital in the immediate future, even if he had to be carried.

Jefferson invited Dolly, Madison, and Anna to make their home with him at the President's House until they could find a place of their own they could buy, rent, or build. There was ample room for them under his bachelor's roof, he said, and waved aside any thought that he was offering them an honor.

For the present, Payne and little Nelly would be left behind at Montpelier since schooling in Washington City was still inadequate. In due time, after good schools had been established and competent private tutors moved there, the children could join the family. Until then they would come to Washington City only for their holidays.

That Dolly herself planned to accompany her husband to Washington City was extraordinary. The wives of most Senators and Congressmen always remained at home, a situation that would persist for many years, and even Cabinet, Supreme Court, and other top-ranking wives were reluctant to make temporary homes for themselves in the primitive new community.

Dolly could have made a strong case for herself by pointing out that the wives of foreign diplomats accredited to the United States government came to Washington City, and that it was essential that the wife of the Secretary of State be on hand. The argument would have been valid, but she felt no need to make it.

She was Mrs. James Madison, and she intended to live with her husband wherever he might be stationed. That was that, and no alternative occurred to her. In two letters to her mother and one to Lucy Washington after Jefferson's March 5 appointment of Madison, she spoke only in terms of moving to Washington City "and enduring" whatever discomforts she might find there. She could have remained behind in comfort at Montpelier, and no one would have thought the worse of her for it, but she loved James Madison too much to be separated from him for long periods, and in addition would have regarded herself as derelict in her duties to him.

Jefferson wrote them a detailed letter after his return to the capital, warning them about areas where they should be on guard against potholes that might break an axle or tip their carriage on its side. The travelers took his advice, and although Madison's physical condition had just started to abate, they left Montpelier on April 29.

Riding by fairly easy stages, they reached Washington

City on May 1 and drove straight to the President's House, where their quarters awaited them. That night they dined for the first time at the Presidential table, and the next morning Madison took the oath of office, which was administered by Federal Judge William Cranch, who happened to be Abigail Adams' brother-in-law.

Madison went to work with such vigor that, according to a letter Jefferson wrote to Monroe, he soon forgot his rheumatism. Meanwhile, Dolly was assuming unexpected duties of her own. Jefferson had asked her to act as his official hostess.

Even if he had not made the request, his widowerhood and that of Vice President Burr would have made her the highest-ranking government wife. That position was doubly confirmed when she took the post of acting First Lady.

She continued to hold the position for the next seven years and ten months of the Jefferson Administration, but her duties were not onerous. On the contrary, they were easy to perform as she was conforming to Jefferson's style of living, which was very informal.

The levees held by John and Abigail Adams had been reminiscent of court receptions at the palaces of European kings, and even the Washingtons had given parties with a royal flavor. Thomas Jefferson changed the atmosphere overnight, saying that the President's House represented the American people at large, that his hospitality should reflect their own customs.

So he gave frequent small dinner parties, usually with no more than a dozen people in attendance, and even his so-called "state" dinners generally were confined to twenty guests. Almost daily he issued spur-of-the-moment invitations to visitors who interested him, inviting them to take potluck with him, and neither Dolly nor the cook ever knew exactly how many people to expect at the table for the next meal.

The atmosphere at the Presidential table was informal, sometimes approaching the chaotic. Jefferson refused to observe protocol, an attitude that eventually caused international repercussions. He himself went wigless, often wore old clothes, and expected his guests to do the same. Ladies of good sense seldom wore new gowns to the President's House. Jefferson paid little attention to what he ate, and after the Madisons moved to their own house, the quality of the meals served under the Presidential roof declined sharply, except on those occasions when Dolly or another lady acted as hostess. Guests were expected to make lively, stimulating contributions to the conversation, and anyone who failed to do so was certain not to be asked again.

The Madisons stayed with the President until autumn, 1801, and Dolly managed to maintain order during her tenure. After she and her husband departed, however, Jefferson's careless attitude sometimes serged on the slovenly, and on one occasion he created a minor scandal by receiving a foreign diplomat in his dressing gown and carpet slippers.

Dolly was well aware of the nuances that governed the lives of statesmen-politicians and their families, and realized she would be criticized as greedy if she monopolized the role of Presidential hostess. So she voluntarily relinquished it on occasion to the wives of other Cabinet members and, less frequently, to the wives of Republican-Democratic Senators and Congressmen. Jefferson did not expect her to assume the obligation on a full-time basis, knowing she would have duties to perform in her own home, but he relied on her to find substitutes when she and her husband went elsewhere—and the President remembered to tell her he was expecting guests. Throughout Jefferson's two terms the Madisons dined with him in private on an average of once each week, and Dolly served as his hostess at all functions she considered important.

The intimacy of the Secretary of State and his wife with the President inevitably caused repercussions among the Federalists, who were anxious to cause as many problems as possible for Jefferson. The American press was still in its infancy, and most newspapers—of every political persuasion—had not yet learned self-restraint and responsibility and, above all, the need to print only accurate information. Many were smear sheets, uninhibited by laws of libel and slander, that were devoted to the goal of destroying the reputations of their enemies.

Soon after President Jefferson took office a number of Federalist newspapers printed a crude poem linking his name with one of his slaves, a woman whose name was variously spelled as Sally Heming or Hemmings. Not only had she been his mistress for years, the verse insisted, but he had sired a number of children by her.

For years thereafter serious historians dismissed the charges, but they happened to be true, as Jefferson's friends well knew. Sally, who remained at Monticello and seldom, if ever, came to Washington City, had accompanied Jefferson and his family to Paris, then had returned voluntarily with them to Virginia, where, at least technically, she had reverted to the position of a slave. Neither Jefferson nor his friends made any reply to the attack.

Dolly Madison was the next Federalist target, scattered newspapers picking up a story that first appeared in Baltimore to the effect that she, too, had been his mistress. The charge was totally false, but Dolly was unaccustomed to such assaults and was badly upset.

Her angry husband told her he would go to Baltimore, find the editor who had been responsible for the piece, and challenge him to a duel. This prospect alarmed her further. Although Madison had served as a colonel in the Army, he disliked hunting, was an indifferent shot, and by temperament was a chess player rather than a soldier.

Madison repeated his intentions to the President, who tried to dissuade him. Since the allegations were without foundation, they would die away if no attention was paid to them. A duel, regardless of its outcome, would create widespread attention, which, in the long run, would do Dolly even more harm.

Secretary Gallatin, whose cool poise under fire Madison admired, supported the President's position, and Governor Monroe added similar advice by letter. Dolly, although mortified and apprehensive, maintained a dignified silence on the matter, not even deigning to mention it in letters to her mother or Lucy. At the same time, she and her husband kept up their close friendship with the President, thus indicating by their actions that they felt contempt for the story.

When the Federalists discovered they could not create a cloud of smoke, much less start a fire, they let the issue drop. They had no proof of their contention and realized they were on untenable ground. Equally important, they were severely criticized by responsible Federalists, men well acquainted with the Madisons and Jefferson, whom they respected regardless of political differences. In Massachusetts the intrepid Abigail Adams indignantly came to Dolly's defense, making her opinions known in no uncertain terms, and the editors were so badly squelched they dropped their allegations two months after creating the issue. The subject was closed, and after November, 1801, it never again appeared in print.

Dolly emerged the victor in her first personal political encounter, which proved to be the only scandal, false or true, in which she was ever involved. Even her husband's most vociferously vocal opponents were compelled to respect her, and throughout the rest of her life no hint of immorality ever smudged her name. Some thought she made too much of social life. The Federalist ladies of New England criticized her interest in clothes, and a few wondered why she and Madison had no children. But her standing was unimpaired.

During the brief period of the flare-up in which her name was coupled with that of Jefferson, an attempt was made through a whispering campaign to discredit her on other, equally dubious grounds. It was said that, because she had borne Madison no children, she was oversexed, this belief being accepted by the ignorant at the beginning of the nineteenth century. But the murmurs were heard no more after the President's detractors abandoned their attempt to attack him through her.

XII

*J*ohn Quincy Adams, son of
the second President of the
United States and himself the sixth, came to Washington
City in 1803 as a newly elected Senator from Massachusetts. Now thirty-six years old, he was more malleable
and subtle than his father, but nevertheless had inherited his parents' rock-ribbed sense of values. Soon after
his arrival in the capital he met Dolly Madison at a
dinner party held at the Dutch legation, and was stunned.
She was "the most beautiful lady in America," he declared, "the liveliest, endowed with the greatest charm,
and possibly was the most sensible." He was not alone
in his opinion, which was shared by almost everyone who
came in contact with her.

Thirty-three years old less than three weeks after her
arrival in Washington City, Dolly was at her most beautiful. Her face reflected character development as well
as physical symmetry, and her figure, although twenty
pounds overweight by the standards of 175 years later,
was regarded by her contemporaries as perfect. She had
emerged completely from her Quaker cocoon, thanks at
least in part to a happy marriage, and she was at home
with everyone, the same with her dressmaker or cook
as she was with the President of the United States or the

head of a foreign legation. Everyone commented on the simplicity and directness of her approach, and her charm was overwhelming.

Her interest in clothes had flagged a trifle during her four-year stay at Montpelier, but now that she was returning to a more sophisticated society, she began to replenish her wardrobe more rapidly. Josephine Bonaparte, whose husband at that time had the title of First Consul of France (in three years he would crown himself emperor), was now the undisputed arbiter of fashion in Europe. Josephine was, more than ever, an advocate of shock value in costuming. She favored gowns that fell in gentle folds with square-cut, very low necklines, and high waists. She liked thin, clinging materials, and in a few years she and Napoleon's sister, Pauline, would startle the world by wearing dresses that they soaked in water every few hours, causing the garments to be plastered to their bodies. For added emphasis they wore no underclothes.

This style was too extreme for the lady from Montpelier, who enjoyed showing off her charms but had no intention of appearing in public half-naked. Dolly's endowments were such that she could dazzle her contemporaries in what came to be known as Empire costumes without dampening her gowns or forgetting to don undergarments.

Her husband, by contrast, became more staid than ever now that he was Secretary of State. Dolly's cousin, Edward Coles, who became President Jefferson's private secretary, later described his initial reactions to Madison, whom he had just met for the first time:

I never knew him to wear any other color than black, his coat being cut in what is termed dress-fashion; his breeches short, with buckles at the knees, black silk stockings, and shoes with strings or long fair boot tops when out in cold weather, or when he rode horseback of which he was fond. His hat was of the shape and fashion usu-

ally worn by gentlemen of his age. He wore powder on his hair, which was dressed full over the ears, tied behind, and brought to a point above the forehead, to cover in some degree his baldness as may be noticed in all the likenesses taken of him. . . .

In height he was about five feet six inches, of small and delicate form, of rather a tawny complexion, bespeaking a sedentary and studious man; his hair was originally of a dark brown color; his eyes were bluish, but not of a bright blue; his form, features, and manner were not commanding, but his conversation exceedingly so and few men possessed so rich a flow of language or so great a fund of amusing anecdotes which were made the more interesting from their being well-timed and well-told. His ordinary manner was simple, modest, bland, and unostentatious, retiring from the throng and cautiously refraining from doing or saying anything to make himself conspicuous.

Young Coles was too much of a gentleman himself and too loyal to family to repeat a comment he heard on all sides from people who had only recently come to know the Madisons. Dolly, according to these sources, was a shrew who dominated her husband. Such stories occasionally drifted back to Dolly, who laughed at them without comment. No denial on her part was necessary. Everyone who knew Madison realized he was a strong-willed man who formed firm opinions and would not be swayed. Unlike many men of the period he did not regard his wife as a chattel, but he did make final decisions, and he expected her to abide by them. It was better, he believed, to obtain her concurrence, but even when she demurred, it was his word that prevailed.

Only rarely did Dolly defy him, and in the choice of her wardrobe she followed her own inclinations. While it was true that, in general, she dressed to please him, she realized he knew nothing about such matters, and consequently she ignored his judgment when it was at variance with her own.

The "Dolly Madison turban" illustrates the kind of dispute that sometimes enlivened the domestic life of the Madisons. Shortly after moving to Washington City Dolly designed a headgear for women that would become her single most important contribution to fashion. She took a three- or four-foot length of material, usually of thin silk, and wound it around her head until it resembled the turban worn by high-ranking members of the Turkish nobility.

It became popular overnight, because ladies quickly discovered it concealed their hair when it needed washing or could not be managed. It also did away with the requirement, resisted by those under forty, that ladies wear wigs or powder their hair on formal occasions.

The style was so popular that it spread to every part of the United States in a few months, crossed the Atlantic to England, and thence made its way to the Continent. Josephine Bonaparte quickly took up the style, guaranteeing its success, and others throughout Europe did the same. Almost a half century later, shortly before Dolly's death, she continued to see the turban in Washington City salons, its longevity partly due to the fact that its appearance could be changed by feathers, jewelry, and other adornments.

Anna Payne, just emerging from her teens, was less than discreet in writing to friends in Virginia, and revealed a lengthy controversy in the family household. James Madison disliked his wife's turbans, insisting they did nothing to improve her appearance. She disagreed, saying he knew nothing about the matter and, presumably, suggesting he save his strength for the conduct of America's troubled relations with other nations. Neither was swayed, both held to their original positions, and a deadlock ensued.

Dolly overcame the impasse by paying no attention to Madison's criticism. She and her friends liked the turbans, which they regarded as both ornamental and practical, and she continued to wear hers on every occasion. Reduced to the helpless position in which countless ordinary husbands had found themselves over the ages, the Secretary of State and future President of the United States kept silent.

During the months the Madisons were guests at the President's House, they did no entertaining on their own, Dolly making herself available to act exclusively as Jefferson's hostess. But Washington City was growing so rapidly that the President, who was aware of everything that happened around him, wrote in October that there were "twice as many buildings in the town" as there had been in August.

In the autumn Dolly found a place suitable for rental, a just-completed house of seventeen rooms off Pennsylvania Avenue. Just prior to moving in they made a trip to Montpelier for various items of furniture and a great many cartons of books they wanted in the capital. They now brought Payne and Nelly back to Washington City with them, arranging to hire tutors until the town's new schools were opened, and the family was reunited.

Several of the family's servants came up to the new house from Virginia, and Dolly launched her own social campaign. Only a few foreign nations maintained legations in the United States in 1801, principal among them being Great Britain, France, Spain, the Netherlands, Sweden, and Prussia, with others gradually joining them over the years. Small staffs were maintained, the customary personnel consisting of a minister who was aided by one or, at the most, two assistants. Virtually all were married and were accompanied by their wives.

The Secretary of State was required to give a continuing series of dinner parties at which all members of the legations and their wives were entertained, and he was also obliged to be present at social functions in the legations. Custom decreed that the President give a dinner for each minister, too, so Dolly and James Madison were required to do double duty.

Dolly's parties at Montpelier had not been elaborate, but she had enjoyed serving a number of European dishes, as well as a growing list of her own, many of which were cooked in wine. Her situation was far different now. She and her husband officially represented the United States, so she felt she should feature American dishes. And she could do none in wine because every drop consumed in the country was imported.

Severely restricted at the outset, she made it her business to learn the regional dishes of every part of the United States. She wrote to friends and acquaintances everywhere, among them Abigail Adams and Mrs. Charles Pinckney of Charleston. The smoked hams and beef sides of Virginia were staples of her table. She adapted many of the recipes sent to her, experimenting herself in her kitchen outbuilding, and by the end of Jefferson's first term the diplomats stationed in Washington City were writing home that Mrs. Madison served the finest meals in America.

Members of the legation staffs were dazzled by Secretary Madison's brilliance and his wife's charm, beauty, and style. But they and their ladies were stunned by the guest list and lack of protocol. Following the example set by Jefferson in the President's House, Dolly maintained a strictly democratic atmosphere, refusing to seat guests according to rank and prohibiting a procession of any kind into the dining room.

No one ever knew who might be a fellow guest. The foreigners expected to meet Cabinet members, Senators, and Congressmen, and did. But the French envoy was startled when he found himself seated opposite a mason who was building a fireplace at his legation. And the British minister's lady was outraged when her fellow guests included her haberdasher and his wife. "Mrs. Madison," she wrote to a friend in London, "is totally lacking in good taste."

The extent to which the Secretary of State and his wife were emulating the President is difficult to determine, but it cannot be forgotten that Madison was a principal architect and prime mover in Jefferson's democratic "revolution," and sincerely concurred in his mentor's view that all men were created equal. He and Dolly could not have been walking blindly in another's footsteps. On the other hand, if Jefferson had not initiated such a policy, it is impossible to guess whether Madison would have been its innovator when he became President. He and Jefferson were so close that no student of history has been able to draw a sharp distinction between their thinking and programs in all eight years of Jefferson's Presidency.

It must suffice that Dolly, after establishing a precedent, held to its principles for the rest of her life. People of every station were given a hearty welcome at her front door, and a Chesapeake Bay fisherman was received with as much warmth as the Marquis de Lafayette, Jerome Bonaparte, the brother of Napoleon, or Viscount Henderson, the proprietor of some of England's largest shipyards. Untutored frontiersmen in grease-stained buckskins sat beside bejeweled foreign ladies wearing gowns of French silk trimmed with Belgian lace, and gentlemen in velvet rubbed shoulders with small-town American women dressed in homespun linsey-woolsey.

An occasional guest was shocked, and even more occasionally one felt insulted. But it was Dolly's genius to put everyone at ease, and most fell so completely under her spell that they enjoyed the thoroughly mixed company. A few Federalist ladies could sniff, and a handful of foreign aristocrats might raise their eyebrows, but the majority of visitors to the Madison house in Washington City or to Montpelier had the time of their lives and were quick to accept when invited again.

Dolly and Madison, although not wealthy by the standards of Boston's shipping tycoon, Governor John Hancock, were comfortably situated. Certainly they recognized the financial gap that separated the Virginia planter from the poor artisan in Philadelphia or New York. But they recognized no social differences, thanks to their conviction that no American was better or worse than any other. A man's standing depended on his integrity and other personal characteristics, not the quantity of gold or silver buried in his cellar.

So Dolly Madison's greatest historical distinction may be something quite apart from the quality of her meals or her charm. For two hundred years Americans have paid lip service to the principles enunciated by Jefferson in the Declaration of Independence. Dolly and her husband believed so completely in these precepts that they lived in accordance with them. Only a very few who came after them did the same, chief among them being Andrew Jackson, the seventh President, who took office twelve years after Madison retired.

It is not true, however, that Dolly was indiscriminate in her choice of guests, as several New England newspapers charged, that she was a hypocrite who invited people of low estate to dine at her table simply because of the stir she would create.

Her standards were exacting, although they applied to men rather than women, in the main, because she lived in a time when most wives were appendages who had no stature in their own right. Her criterion was simple. Aside from those whom duty required her to entertain, she invited only guests who had something positive to offer the rest of the company.

Making her position plain in her subsequent correspondence with Anna over many years, Dolly insisted that she and her husband welcomed no one but men of intellect, charm, or talent. Occasionally there were a few others, but they, too, had to be men of integrity. An individual's wealth meant nothing, nor did his table manners, even though she might cringe inwardly if a careless guest left a permanent wine or coffee stain on one of her tablecloths of imported linen and lace.

Because of her husband's position, first as Secretary of State and then as President, Dolly was a trend setter. Countless Republican-Democratic ladies in every state enthusiastically followed her example, and for more than three decades, until Jackson's retirement from the Presidency in 1837, at which time other values began to reassert themselves, the great American experiment was an unqualified social success. Dolly's courage carried the "revolution" of Jefferson and Madison even farther than they may have hoped.

Domestic political considerations appear to have been irrelevant to Jefferson and the Madisons, who neither publicized their attitude nor tried in other ways to win increased popularity with the electorate. They were naïve, however, in spite of their sincerity, and their unique approach almost inevitably created complications.

The diplomat, both personally and professionally, is a conservative man, cautious and habitually enamored of protocol, his protective armor. Perhaps the President and his Secretary of State knew their informality would cause trouble, but did not care. Whatever they may have thought in private, Dolly suddenly found herself the central figure in a diplomatic incident that had widespread repercussions.

XIII

*I*n the spring of 1803 a new minister representing His Britannic Majesty arrived in Washington City. According to Rufus King and James Monroe, the two American diplomats who had known him best in London, Anthony Merry was a sensible, sober, hard-working man. Neither realized perhaps that he suffered from a severe sense of inferiority, caused in part by the fact that he was a commoner who had worked his way up the Foreign Office ladder, while most of his colleagues of equal rank were aristocrats.

Merry's real problem, however, was his wife, who towered over the slender minister. Mrs. Merry was a compulsive talker, a masculine woman with a deep voice and an insatiable demand for the spotlight. She wore bright-colored gowns that called attention to her bulk, and on most social occasions she appeared in the better part of the gaudy jewelry she had spent a lifetime collecting.

According to the legation secretary, Augustus J. Foster, the Merrys were fish out of water in America. The minister was a plodder, almost totally lacking in imagination, and was out of sorts because London had granted him no funds for extensive entertaining. He was bothered, too, by the fact that in a town as primitive as Washington City there was no place where he could entertain guests other than his own home. Mrs. Merry, who kept him on a short leash, was a virago who intimidated her servants and gave so many orders to the legation secretary that there were times he almost thought she was the minister. She was appalled, as was Foster, by so-called American society. She regarded all Americans as savages, and she loathed the women in particular because so many were the daughters of clerks, innkeepers, and boardinghouse proprietors.

The potential for trouble existed from the time of the Merrys' arrival. The minister was miffed after his first visit to the President's House to present his credentials, when Jefferson received him in bathrobe and slippers. Merry immediately lodged a complaint with Secretary Madison, saying he had been subjected to a deliberate slight.

The amused Madison shrugged off the minister's diatribe. The President had intended no insult, he explained, and had been similarly attired when the representative of Denmark had called on him. Merry refused to be mollified. He held the second rank in the Foreign Service, and consequently was entitled to a greater display of Presidential courtesy than the Dane, who held the third rank.

Madison thought the matter was too trivial to be pursued, and had no idea that Merry continued to simmer. Quiet reigned until December 2, when the President gave a diplomatic dinner, by which time the Merrys had made it their business to learn that at similar functions President Adams had always offered his arm to the British minister's wife as the guests filed into the dining room.

Dinner was duly announced, and Jefferson offered his arm to Dolly, whom he seated on his right. The outraged Mrs. Merry watched him compound the felony by giving the place on his left to the wife of Carlos Martinez d'Yrujo, the Spanish minister. This lady happened to be an American, the former Sally McKean, so Mrs. Merry jumped to the conclusion that the President was going out of his way to honor his compatriots at the expense of distinguished foreign guests.

Secretary Madison rescued the seething Mrs. Merry and seated her between Yrujo and himself. In the scramble for seats Merry fared even worse than his wife. He tried to take the place beside Mme. Yrujo, but was literally pushed aside by a member of the House of Representatives whose boots were caked with dried mud.

The final blow was more than the Merrys could bear. Jefferson offered the privilege of making the first toast of the evening to Louis Pichon, the charming and gallant French minister. It didn't matter to the Merrys that Pichon, one of the few men in Washington City capable of engaging with the President in talk on intellectual matters, happened to be Jefferson's friend. Britain was at war with France, and the Merrys were convinced they were being subjected to yet another deliberate insult by the highest official in the United States.

The next morning the British minister appeared at Secretary Madison's office to lodge a formal protest. Spurred by his wife's determination, Merry delivered a long, rambling speech. Madison listened in silence. Then, privately deciding that most of the charges were so absurd they required no rebuttal, he confined his own remarks to one. At the President's dinner table, he said, "a liberal oblivion of all hostile relations ought to take place." For a few hours ministers should ignore the unfortunate state of war that existed between their respective nations.

Perhaps Merry would have subsided had it not been for his wife, who remained unmollified and was prepared to renew the battle. She had her chance a few weeks later, when Dolly and her husband gave a formal dinner attended by members of the diplomatic corps and the Cabinet. Pichon had seen his own wife and Sally Yrujo treated with a measure of ceremony under the Madison roof, and expected the Secretary of State to disarm Mrs. Merry by giving her precedence.

But Dolly and her husband felt this could not be done without making it appear that they were abandoning the President. Under no circumstances would they allow any of their actions to be intended as disloyal or discourteous to Jefferson, and it is possible, as Pichon believed, that they were annoyed by the fuss the Merrys had already created.

Whatever their motives, Anglo-American discord deepened when dinner was announced and the Secretary of State offered his arm to Mrs. Gallatin. This unexpected gesture created what Pichon called "a sort of derangement in the salon." For a few moments guests milled around in confusion, but it could not have been accidental that Pichon found himself escorting Dolly to the table.

Couples quickly sorted themselves out as they marched into the dining room. Mrs. Merry was ignored by gentlemen who didn't know how she might react to this new "insult" and had no desire to be on the receiving end of a tirade. So she stood alone in the salon, red-faced and furious, until her husband was compelled to come to her rescue, himself taking her to the table.

The next day Merry delivered an even stiffer protest.

Secretary Madison realized that Merry's Foreign Office superiors might believe that the United States was using the incident to signal its displeasure with British controls of international trade during the fight with Napoleon. Only twenty-one years had passed since the signing of the 1783 peace treaty with the United States, and relations between the young nation and the mother country were still delicate.

Dolly was credited with conceiving an idea intended to bring the ridiculous dinner-table feud to an end. She and her husband would give yet another party, and would announce in advance that it was being held in honor of the Merrys. She wrote a formal invitation, and quickly received a formal acceptance from Mrs. Merry. The relieved Secretary of State believed that the end of the artificial crisis was within sight, and that soon it would be possible to hold serious discussions with the British minister.

The night of the party came and the company assembled, but there was no sign of the guests of honor. Dolly maintained a surface calm that everyone present admired, but her husband's growing tension was obvious, and he withdrew farther and farther into a cold shell.

Finally, an hour after the dinner was scheduled to begin, Anthony Merry made his belated appearance. He was alone, and offered no excuse for his tardiness as he joined the group.

Dolly felt it was her duty as the hostess to inquire after Mrs. Merry's whereabouts.

"She is indisposed," the British minister said, and did not explain.

The snub was openly deliberate, but Dolly reacted with aplomb. She smiled, expressing the hope that Mrs. Merry would recover soon from her temporary infirmity, and did not mention the matter again.

Had the British minister and his wife been satisfied with their victory, there would have been no additional repercussions. But the vindictive Mrs. Merry was not yet satisfied, and events in Europe strengthened her hand, or so she believed. Britain was tightening her alliance with Spain in opposition to Napoleon, and Merry proposed to Yrujo that they stand together in a show of solidarity that would humiliate the French minister as well as teach the upstart Americans a lesson. Sally Yrujo, who had been taking herself increasingly seriously since her marriage to a Spanish aristocrat, was eager to cooperate.

The British and Spanish ministers paid a joint call on the Secretary of State and laid down an ultimatum. They demanded that the President give alternating precedence to their wives at future diplomatic dinners, and said that unless such a firm promise was given, the ladies would boycott all functions at the President's House.

Madison, who privately said he was nauseated by what he regarded as a "frivolous farce," which he had described on one occasion as "a foolish circumstance of etiquet," reported the Anglo-Spanish stand to the President.

Jefferson and Madison agreed they could not allow Mrs. Merry and Mme. Yrujo to put the United States in a ridiculous light. So Dolly, acting on the President's behalf, issued an invitation to members of the diplomatic corps and their wives to dine with Jefferson.

Mrs. Merry and Sally Yrujo made good their threat and absented themselves from the President's House.

Meanwhile Minister Merry was writing long, angry reports to London, and Madison became seriously concerned that America's relations with Britain might worsen.

Merry soon found fresh ammunition for the private war his wife was waging. Napoleon's young brother Jerome came to the United States on a visit, and to the surprise of those unfamiliar with Bonaparte impetuosity, married Elizabeth Patterson, a lovely Baltimore heiress. She happened to be the niece of Secretary of the Navy Robert Smith and his brother Samuel, one of the more influential Republican-Democrats in the House of Representatives.

President Jefferson gave a dinner party for the bride and groom and, not realizing he was adding fuel to the fire, escorted Elizabeth Bonaparte to the dinner table. Anthony Merry and his wife were not present, to be sure, but they heard the details the following day, and were furious. The President, they were convinced, was doing everything in his power to denigrate the social status of the representative of the British Crown in America.

A few nights later French Minister Pichon gave a dinner for the newlyweds, and the entire diplomatic corps came to his house. Acting with due deliberation, he offered his arm to Dolly Madison, whose husband wrote to Monroe that Mrs. Merry looked as though she were "suffering an apoplectic stroke."

The climactic battle of the diplomatic war was waged in early February, 1804. Robert and Samuel Smith gave a ball in honor of their niece and her husband, and it promised to be the most glamorous social event in the short history of Washington City. The President accepted an invitation, and so did everyone else of consequence in town.

Mrs. Merry stunned the assemblage, but not in the manner she intended. Wearing a gown of dark blue with a white train and yards of additional white draped over her ample bosom, she was bedecked in diamonds, including a tiara, a necklace, a brooch, earrings, a solitaire ring, and two bracelets.

Elizabeth Bonaparte appeared in a gown of dampened muslin that clung to her body in the style made popular by her relative-by-marriage, Josephine, whom she hadn't met. The guests were so shocked that no one had the courage to gape at her openly.

Among the last to arrive were Secretary and Mrs. Madison. Dolly was dressed in a gown of ivory satin with a square-cut neckline, and two ostrich plumes rose from her turban. The ladies gasped in admiration, and the smiling gentlemen started to applaud, but were discouraged by Dolly herself. By comparison the guest of honor looked tawdry, and Mrs. Merry looked ludicrous.

The *National Intelligencer* reported Dolly's triumph at length, and even saluted Elizabeth Bonaparte for her daring. Mrs. Merry was ignored, but she knew she had made a laughingstock of herself.

Mrs. Merry could tolerate no more, particularly as she was afraid an account of her debacle might appear in the London newspapers. She goaded her husband into paying a formal call on the Secretary of State and making an official protest. Until now the dispute had been social, but that visit transformed it into a diplomatic problem of the first magnitude.

Madison, in spite of his disgust, treated the subject with solemnity. Mrs. Merry, he said, would have "received the first attention" at an informal social gathering under his roof, but she had chosen not to attend such an event. At formal or official functions he would not and could not "deviate from the established course."

Speaking for the record, Madison emphasized that different social standards prevailed in different countries. Precedence in England, he realized, was based on heredity, but this was not true elsewhere. Ecclesiastical rank took precedence in Rome, and military rank was accorded top honors at the Imperial Russian court. Domestic standing came first in Berlin, the capital of Prussia, no matter how exalted a foreigner might be. The United States was establishing her own customs, and here the rule of *pêle-mêle,* or that of every guest for himself, was paramount. Americans were entitled to live as they saw fit, and foreigners dwelling in their midst had to respect their ways, a requirement on foreigners everywhere.

Never losing his poise during the discussion, Madison nevertheless made it clear that nothing would be done to alleviate the situation. No insult was directed at Great Britain or her principal representative in the United States, but if Merry chose to believe otherwise, that was his privilege. Ushering his guest to the door without giving him any of the satisfaction he had sought, the Secretary of State returned to his desk and wrote a long account of the meeting to Monroe. Apologetic and exasperated, he concluded, "I blush at having put so much trash on paper."

Merry was not content to let the matter rest and seized an opportunity when invited to a bachelor dinner at the President's House. He could not attend, he said, until he received instructions from his government. Then he persuaded the pliable Yrujo to take an identical stand.

It was the turn of Jefferson and Madison to become angry. Pichon, who sat next to the President at the dinner, wrote to Foreign Minister Talleyrand in Paris that Jefferson felt the United States had been affronted: "'It is unheard of,' he told me, 'that a foreign minister has need of the permission of his court to sit down at the table of the head of a state—I shall be highly honored when the king of England is good enough to let Mr. Merry come and eat my soup.'"

Soon there was soothing news from England. Minister Monroe made it his business to find out the British government's reaction to Merry's complaints, and learned they were being ignored. Holding Napoleon at bay and trying to prevent other nations from aiding him, advertently or otherwise, was a full-time occupation that made it impossible for anyone in authority to give serious weight to Merry's nitpicking.

Dolly's poise throughout the long crisis had matched that of her husband. Although her private opinion of the Merrys was unfavorable, she confided in no one except Anna. She was always polite, never cold, when her path crossed that of the Merrys, and she invariably made it her business to engage them in conversation.

She was the symbol of their discontent, but her own position as the wife of the Secretary of State and the official hostess to the President forced them to remain on speaking terms with her. Had they snubbed her, as they secretly wished, according to Sally Yrujo, Madison would have been justified in demanding Merry's recall.

That, however, was the last thing James Madison wanted. In spite of his irritation over the Merrys' silly social posturing, he wrote repeatedly to Monroe that he regarded the British minister as the best representative London could have in Washington City. Merry's diligence and lack of imagination were assets that served the United States. He sent literal reports to his superiors and consequently could be relied upon to transmit the precise American views on various affairs of state to the Foreign Office.

Had Dolly known the Merrys in private life she might have thought their rebuffs intolerable. But her husband found the minister useful, so she acted accordingly, and when Monroe reported that Merry was receiving no support in London, she extended the couple another invitation to dinner. She stressed its informality, a signal that they would be treated on an unofficial basis—that is, the American concept of protocol would be observed.

Merry was in a difficult position, and he knew it, so his wife swallowed her pride and accepted the invitation. A smiling host and hostess greeted them and accorded them every courtesy. Madison made a point of offering his arm to Mrs. Merry when the party went to the dinner table.

In spite of the efforts made by the Madisons, the Merrys were offended. Dolly had attempted to gather a lively group, and in her innocence she had invited one of the most charming, energetic couples she knew—Washington City's only haberdasher and his wife.

Mrs. Merry was incapable of understanding American democracy and felt certain the haberdasher's presence was a deliberate insult to her own upper-class background.

Legation Secretary Foster told his mother the story in a long letter and, reflecting the views of the Merrys, concluded by saying that the United States was "indeed a country not fit for a dog."

XIV

*L*ife in Washington City was pleasant for the Madisons, aside from their irritation over the dinner-table war. The Secretary walked the equivalent of two city blocks to work each day, and for a time, until a separate structure was built for the State Department, he shared quarters with the War Department.

A few months after moving into their rented house, located on what would become F Street, NW, Dolly and her husband decided to buy the place that would be their home for eight years. They wanted to make a number of improvements, and the builder sold it to them for $2,375, which was then regarded as a high price.

Under Dolly's supervision two new cellars were added, one for wine and the other for coal. An indoor water closet was constructed, the dining room was paneled in walnut, and a coach house was built in the rear, adjacent to the stable.

A number of retail shops and service establishments were opening on the roads off Pennsylvania Avenue, between the Capitol and the President's House, gradually making life somewhat easier for the town's permanent residents. A shoemaker located his workroom next door to a printer, and a block away a tailor had set up shop. A second tailor and the haberdasher occupied nearby houses, and several women who took in washing opened their doors as the boardinghouses occupied by civil servants and members of the Congress proliferated. Dolly could do her marketing at either of two greengrocers, a butcher shop, and a small meat market. The only baker sold exclusively to boardinghouse owners; permanent occupants of private homes baked their own bread.

A store that sold books, pamphlets, and stationery opened near the President's House, and both Jefferson and Madison became steady patrons. A small general store and a dry-goods shop were in business near the Capitol, and a year or so later a second dry-goods shop opened near the President's House.

An older community, Georgetown, was located in the Federal District that had been created as the nation's capital, but it was too far from the seat of government to be regarded as part of Washington City. Not until James Madison became President would the forests and many swamps that separated the two communities begin to disappear as new roads and houses, churches and schools were built.

In the summer of 1801, the first that officials of the government spent in Washington City, it became painfully evident that the site chosen for the capital of the United States left a great deal to be desired. The heat was blistering, the humidity was stultifying, and the swarms of flies, mosquitoes, and gnats that bred in the swamps added to the misery of town dwellers.

The summer weather proved to be too much for the man who worked harder than anyone else in Washington City, James Madison. In addition to being responsible for the State Department, he was President Jefferson's closest collaborator and confidant in virtually every aspect of government operations. He had so little free time that only occasionally could he accompany Dolly and the children on the morning ride through the woods that the entire family enjoyed.

In mid-July, 1801, he collapsed, his ailment being diagnosed as a "bilious attack." Dolly believed the Washington City weather and overwork were responsible and decided that the family should go to Montpelier for the months of August and September. Madison demurred, but Jefferson regarded the advice as sensible and urged his friend to leave. Madison's sense of duty was so strong he refused.

Dolly took charge, informing him the family would depart on July 30 and that she intended to remain in Virginia indefinitely unless he went with her. Madison buckled in the face of her firm stand, consoling himself with the thought that he would be able to work at Montpelier.

A precedent was set, and for the next decade and a half, throughout Madison's tenure as Secretary of State and two terms as President, he and Dolly spent every August and September in Virginia. She sometimes persuaded him to leave Washington City for a portion of July, too, but he was adamant in his insistence that he would return to the capital each year no later than the beginning of October.

Familiar patterns were quickly resumed at Montpelier, and if work kept Madison isolated in his study for long periods, making it difficult for him to visit friends and relatives, they came more frequently to his house. Dolly entertained regularly. She wrote to Lucy that there were guests for dinner almost every day. Other Cabinet members and their wives, members of the Congress, and foreign diplomats seldom came to Montpelier, however, so most visitors were either relatives or personal friends. With ample help available, the hostess was under little strain.

The President absented himself from Washington City during the hot months, too, so he and his Secretary of State maintained their custom of exchanging frequent visits. Dolly always accompanied her husband to Monticello, and while the men conferred, she spent her time with Jefferson's daughters or any guests who might be there. The twenty-five mile drive was no hardship, and she wanted to be on hand when her husband was not working. It was typical of their relationship that she thought first of him.

The Monroes were in Virginia until January, 1803, when the recently retired governor of Virginia was given a special position in the State Department. Madison sent him off to Europe on what was, in effect, a triple assignment: Monroe was made minister extraordinary to Spain, with authority to initiate negotiations for the purchase of the Floridas; he was given the rank of minister extraordinary to France, where he was to join Minister Robert R. Livingston in an attempt to purchase New Orleans; and, finally, he was to obtain as much information as possible on the attitudes of the British government.

For the better part of two centuries the various admirers of Jefferson, Madison, Livingston, and Monroe have claimed that their favorite was responsible for the American acquisition of the vast Louisiana Territory from France, the single most important addition to the nation's borders in her history. The President and his Secretary of State worked together in such close harmony that it is impossible to give credit to one without bestowing a palm on the other. Livingston and Monroe each claimed the full responsibility, but both exaggerated.

The men really responsible for what came to be known as the Louisiana Purchase were Napoleon and his astute foreign secretary, Talleyrand, who was the first to mention the subject to the startled and pleased American envoys. Their reasons for selling the vast tract were fundamental. France had just recently acquired the territory from Spain and had not yet established firm control there. Even more important, Napoleon was concentrating on the European theater of operations in his struggle with Great Britain. His armies were supreme on the Continent, but the British navy still controlled the seas, and he could put up no more than a token response if his enemy seized the territory. He preferred to be rid of a vulnerable burden.

An agreement was reached on April 29, 1803. The United States would pay the sum of $15 million and in return would take possession of more than 820,000 square miles, increasing the territory of the United States by approximately 140 percent. All or parts of thirteen future states were included, and America was transformed overnight from a small Atlantic-seaboard nation to a great power that spread across half the continent.

When news of the Louisiana Purchase reached Washington City in July, most government officials were stunned. Secretary of the Treasury Gallatin protested that the price was exorbitant, but Secretary of State Madison, who immediately organized surveys of the new territory, spoke of the "Empire of Liberty," one of his more colorful phrases.

New Orleans, almost as large as New York or Philadelphia, was the most cosmopolitan city in North America, and an excited Dolly Madison wrote at length to Anna, who was paying a visit to their mother and Lucy. They would go to New Orleans for the annexation ceremonies, she said, and if Madison could be persuaded to take a holiday, she hoped they would travel by boat up the Mississippi River.

In the first flush of their joint enthusiasm for the venture, Madison may have agreed to his wife's plans. But he was far too busy to make a journey that would take two to three weeks by ship and at least twice that time by an overland route. The visit to New Orleans had to be postponed.

Dolly did not abandon the idea, however, and kept the project alive as long as her husband served as Secretary of State. She was forced to shelve it during his Presidency, particularly because of the fighting that took place in the vicinity of New Orleans during the final phase of the War of 1812.

She revived the plan when she and her husband retired to Montpelier to stay. She longed to visit the city where French and Spanish were spoken, where the food was unlike that served in any part of the United States she knew, and where even the styles were unique. Her dreams were not realized. Madison was tired after his many years of service to his country and was content to stay at home. Of course Dolly stayed with him, but to the end of her days she was eager to talk about New Orleans with visitors from Louisiana.

On one occasion, when she was an old lady, she listened to a detailed description of a ball recently held in New Orleans. Then she sighed. "If I were young again," she said, "I would go there to stay."

While awaiting the fulfillment of her dream, she had to be content with the more mundane. Late in 1802 Washington City's first public drinking-and-eating establishment was opened a short distance from the Capitol. It was called the Oyster House, and the low prices charged for whiskey, rum, and brandywine assured its immediate success. Most of its patronage was male, and although women were admitted, it was said that the majority were prostitutes from Baltimore.

Certainly no lady had ever set foot in the place when Dolly decided, about three months after the Oyster House opened, that she wanted to go there for a platter of seafood. Her startled husband did not protest, knowing he would lose the argument. Instead he sent a State Department clerk to the proprietor with a message to the effect that Secretary and Mrs. Madison would dine there the following day.

The owner took the hint and put his house in order. When Dolly walked in the next day, the main taproom was spotless, with fresh sawdust thrown on the floor. The trollops from Baltimore were conspicuously missing, and the male customers, who sometimes behaved so boisterously that it was necessary to summon the constabulary, conversed in low tones.

Dolly was pleased. She announced that the oysters were delicious and promised to return. The clientele of the tavern changed almost at once, and soon other ladies began to appear with their husbands. Excessive drinking was discouraged, women of easy virtue were barred, and Dolly, who apparently had no idea she was responsible for the transformation of the place, returned many times for a quiet meal. Two other taverns were opened to meet the demands of the raucous and the earthy.

Two years after the beginning of the first Jefferson Administration there were enough wives and daughters of government officials, foreign diplomats, and local merchants in Washington City to form a lively society. The queen of the town was Dolly Madison, but her reign did not depend on her twin positions as wife of the Secretary of State and hostess for the President.

She drew people to her because she was charming to everyone, showed no favoritism, and was not impressed by rank. Margaret Bayard Smith, who despised the haughty, referred to her again and again as "natural, never assuming airs." If all men were equal, as she and her husband believed, they deserved equal hospitality. It was her generosity, Mrs. Smith wrote, that made Washington City the social as well as the political capital of the United States. The wives of prominent men from Boston and New York, Charleston and Philadelphia, and even New Orleans came to Washington City with their husbands, although the boardinghouses were crowded and travel conditions crude. They returned home with increased stature because they could tell their friends they had dined as the guests of Mrs. Madison.

But there were limits to the hospitality Dolly was willing to extend. In 1801 a visitor from New York, Matthew L. Davis, arrived at Montpelier uninvited. A close associate of Vice President Burr, he was seeking a political post in the new administration. Even before Dolly learned the reason for his visit she was cold to him, and when her husband informed her that Davis was a job seeker, her chill became deeper. Davis was so uncomfortable he cut short his stay and rode to Monticello, where another icy reception awaited him, the President informing him that he never discussed political matters at home.

In the summer of 1802 a new friend, who was a stranger to Virginia, had an opportunity to record her impressions of Montpelier. The Madisons' Washington City neighbors were Dr. William Thornton, director of the patent office, a State Department subsidiary, and his French-born wife, Anne Marie. They were invited to the Virginia estate, and Mrs. Thornton wrote about the place in her diary:

It is in a wild and romantic country very generally covered with fine flourishing timber. The house is plain but grand, rendered more pleasing by displaying a taste for the arts which is rarely to be found in such retired and remote situations. The house is on a height commanding an extensive view of the blue ridge, which by constant variation in the appearance of the clouds, and consequently of the mountains, form a very agreeable and varied object, sometimes appearing very distant, sometimes much separated and distinct, and often like rolling waves.

Guests were treated casually, in the English manner, at Montpelier. Those who arose early were served tea in their rooms and had a standing invitation to join their host and hostess, Anna, Payne, and Nelly for a ride through the woods. Those who wanted to sleep later joined the family and the other guests in the dining room for breakfast at nine.

The Secretary usually retired to his study after breakfast, and wasn't seen again for the better part of the day. Guests did not intrude there. They joined him only when asked to do so at a specific time for a specific purpose.

Each day Dolly paid a visit to her mother-in-law's quarters, usually remaining for an hour, and then spent another hour with Payne and Nelly. The children were subjected to a maternal "homily" on whatever subject came to Dolly's mind at the moment, and when Madison could spare the time, he lectured them, too. Like all good parents of the period, the couple acted in accordance with the customs of the day, and it did not occur to either to share their activities with the children.

The guests were free to do as they pleased, and most occupied themselves by walking in the woods, riding, watching the view from the portico, or fishing in nearby streams until midafternoon. Then the entire party reassembled for a leisurely dinner. Thereafter the hostess and guests retired to the parlor, where the host also joined them when he was not inundated by paperwork. When President Jefferson was present, he and Madison usually went into the study, and the guests did not see them again that evening.

Tea was served around 7 or 8 P.M., and Dolly proudly served fresh and preserved fruits grown on the estate, home-cured ham, and bread baked that day in the Montpelier kitchen. Wine was available for those who wanted it, but neither the host nor hostess drank in the evening. Years later Dolly explained that wine consumed before bedtime gave both of them heartburn. The host and hostess retired around ten, but those guests who wanted to con-

(149)

tinue their conversation in the parlor were free to remain there as late as they wished.

Augustus Foster, who, at the climax of the dinner-table war, had called America a land not fit for a dog, stopped at Montpelier en route to Monticello during the last year of Jefferson's first term as President and was impressed in spite of himself. "The Secretary of State," he later wrote, "was a man of good family and had a considerable estate. No man had a higher reputation among his acquaintances for probity and good honorable feeling, while he was allowed on all sides to be a gentleman in his manners as well as a man of public virtue."

The Montpelier woods, Foster wrote, were "very fine," but he denigrated the gardens of which Dolly was so proud. In his opinion there were no formal gardens at Montpelier, but he was measuring them by the yardstick applied to the gardens at England's great estates.

The heat in Virginia's lowlands was unbearable in summer, Foster said, so ladies of quality preferred "a high situation" for their walks. The woods near the main house were filled with wild turkeys, which supplied game for the Montpelier table.

Admitting that the house and view were beautiful, Foster nevertheless deplored the sights and smells of the surrounding countryside. Apparently it did not occur to him that, unlike the estates of aristocrats in England, Montpelier was a working farm.

Madison, in the Englishman's opinion, was "better informed" than President Jefferson, and "moreover a social, jovial and good-humored companion full of anecdote, and sometimes matter of a loose description relating to old times, but oftener of a political and historical interest. . . . He was a little man, with small features wizened when I saw him, but occasionally lit up with a good-natured smile."

He was less charitable in his comments on Dolly, but

nevertheless saluted her: "She was a very handsome woman and tho' an uncultivated mind and fond of gossiping, was so perfectly good-tempered and good-humored that she rendered her husband's house as far as depended on her agreeable to all parties."

Thanks to Dolly's intrepidity in establishing and maintaining a family home in the wilds of Washington City, the wives of many Senators and members of the House of Representatives followed her example in the second year of the Jefferson Administration. Those who could find no private dwellings lived in boardinghouses until houses of their own could be built for them. The boom-town atmosphere increased, and Congressmen with eligible daughters realized that a community filled with prominent bachelors was a perfect place to live.

Invitations to the houses of the President and the Secretary of State were eagerly sought, and Dolly obliged the newcomers. First she persuaded Jefferson to give an informal reception for Congressional families, and then she followed this party with a similar affair of her own.

So many dinners, assemblies, and balls were given in the winter of 1801–1802 that Margaret Bayard Smith was harried. She wrote that she and her husband rarely spent an evening at home, and sometimes they were invited to as many as three or four affairs in one night. The Madisons were the prime targets of every hostess in town, particularly as Jefferson made it a matter of principle to accept invitations only from old friends at very private functions.

Dolly was inundated, but rejected many more than she accepted. Her husband's time was valuable, his health was precious, and his attendance at affairs given by the foreign diplomats was obligatory. So she protected him by engaging in a careful process of selection. She knew hard feelings would be caused if she and Madison appeared at one Congressman's house but refused to go to another, so she accepted only those extended by the leaders of the political parties.

Realizing she would be criticized if she confined their social life to Washington City's aristocracy, she made it a point to attend an occasional small dinner given by a merchant or innkeeper. No one could accuse Jefferson's closest associate of failing to practice what the administration preached.

Thanks to a lucky accident in timing, the news of the Louisiana Purchase reached the capital late in the day on July 3, 1803, and Jefferson, with Dolly's help, gave an impromptu reception on the grounds of the President's House the next afternoon, followed by an outdoor Independence Day dinner for more than a hundred guests. The celebration was the most spirited ever held in the town, and the last guests did not go home until dawn. The President retired at midnight and Secretary Madison dozed in a guest bedroom, but Dolly remained the animated hostess until the end, finally rousing her husband after the last of the visitors had gone.

The return of Jefferson and the Madisons to Virginia during the summer curtailed Washington City's social life for several months, but the rejoicing over the Louisiana Purchase resumed in the autumn. That season may have been the gayest and most active during Jefferson's two terms as President.

The Madisons did more entertaining than previously, and posterity is indebted to Senator William Plumer of New Hampshire for a description of one meal he ate at their house:

An excellent dinner. The round of Beef of which the Soup is made is called Bouilli: *It had in [it] the dish spices and something of the sweet herb and Garlic kind, and a rich gravy. It is very much boiled, and is still very good. We had a dish with what appeared to be Cabbage, much boiled, then cut in long strings and somewhat mashed; in the middle a large Ham, with the cabbage around. It looked like our country dishes of Bacon and Cabbage, with the Cabbage mashed up, after being boiled till sodden and turned dark. The Dessert good; much as usual, except two dishes which appeared like Apple pie, in the form of the half of a musk-melon, the flat side down, tops creased deep, and the color a dark brown.*

Plumer was more flattering to Dolly than Foster: "As profusion so repugnant to foreign customs arose from the happy circumstance of the abundance and prosperity of our country, she did not hesitate to sacrifice the delicacy of European taste, for the less elegant, but more liberal fashion of Virginia."

Perhaps the most important social event in the spring of 1804 was the marriage of Anna Payne to a handsome, promising young member of the House of Representatives, Richard Cutts, of Massachusetts' Maine District. He was one of the few Republican-Democrats from New England in the Congress and was a great admirer of Secretary Madison. Anna would not have married any man who failed to support her brother-in-law, whom she regarded as a father.

Madison gave the bride away, Dolly was her sister's matron of honor, and both the Payne and Madison families were in attendance. So many relatives crowded into the little Episcopal church that the wedding had to be kept private, with President Jefferson one of the few outsiders in attendance. Dolly wept copiously throughout the ceremony, and her husband was heard to clear his throat repeatedly.

A reception was held at the Madison house, with refreshments served on the lawn, a threat of rain failing to materialize. Everyone of consequence in Washington City, and many who were not, showed up. The President and his Cabinet, the Justices of the Supreme Court, Senators, and Congressmen represented the United States, as did a number of local tradespeople, boardinghouse keepers, and the blacksmith who had shod Anna's mare. They thought the party was a fine affair.

Guests from the foreign legations, however, stared in wonder, marveling at the customs of the Americans. For all practical purposes Anna was the foster-daughter of the nation's crown prince, but the simplicity of the reception was staggering.

Most of the gifts presented to the bridal couple were handmade, including embroidered towels, pin cushions, and original paintings and poems written for the occasion. Augustus Foster was stunned to discover that it was considered bad taste to present the bridal pair with expensive gifts.

Two pits had been excavated in the backyard, and in them a side of beef and a side of venison had been cooking over bright coals since the previous day. Huge loaves of round "pure wheat" bread and cornbread had been baked in the Madison kitchen that morning, and a variety of pickled vegetables and other relishes were available on tables. The Americans thoroughly enjoyed early corn from South Carolina, roasted in the coals, but the Europeans found maize alien to their taste. Other tables were piled high with cakes, pastries, and pies.

Only two beverages were served, the more popular being a potent rum and Madeira punch. The other, "a collation of pressed fruit juices, sweetened with sugar," was favored by the children and the more timid ladies.

The bride and groom were almost forgotten, with a large group forming around President Jefferson and another surrounding Secretary Madison. Dolly, attired in a gown described by Margaret Bayard Smith as "elegant in the simplicity of its line, lacking in pleats and falling in graceful folds to her ankles," was a never-ending source of attention as she moved from house to garden through the throngs, making certain there were no hitches. She was not too busy to attend to Madison's mother and her own, the two old ladies sitting apart from the crowds in a sunny corner protected from the wind.

A final shock awaited the foreigners when the bride and groom drove off in a carriage that had been surreptitiously and grotesquely decorated by some of the guests. The bridal pair were pelted with "all manner of soft objects," and among those throwing balls of colored cotton and confetti at them were the President, the Secretary of State, and his lady. Truly, the foreigners thought, America was a land of barbarians.

But Dolly, in a letter written to the honeymooning Anna in Virginia, reported that "everyone had a grand time; all were agreed it was a lovely, happy wedding."

XV

*O*n July 11, 1804, Vice President Burr won eternal infamy by killing Alexander Hamilton in a duel and warrants for his arrest were issued by New York and New Jersey. Dolly Madison made no recorded comment, either in public or private, that indicated her opinion of the man who had tried to woo her.

The collapse of Burr's reputation in no way affected the standing of the President, whose first term was drawing to a close. It was taken for granted that he would run for reelection, and Secretary of State Madison, who made an intensive political survey on his behalf, assured him that a low-key campaign would suffice.

The 1804 election was the first in which members of the Electoral College would cast separate ballots for President and Vice President, and the Republican-Democrats, who were enthusiastically unanimous in their support of Jefferson, selected George Clinton of New York as his running mate.

Jefferson and Madison were now spending much of their time dealing with the piratical rulers of North Africa's Barbary states, who were exacting tribute from American merchant ships, and the President was too busy to campaign for reelection. The Secretary of State managed to make a few token speeches on his superior's behalf, but the outcome was taken so much for granted that Dolly remained behind in Washington City when her husband went off on brief trips.

The election took place in November, and when the ballots were counted at the beginning of the next month, the optimism of the administration was justified. Jefferson defeated his Federalist opponent, Charles C. Pinckney, by an overwhelming electoral vote of 162 to 14.

The government leaders made no changes of consequence in their way of life, and Jefferson's second inauguration, on March 4, 1805, was a quiet affair. Dolly once again acted as the official hostess at the reception given at the President's House, and unexpected developments forced her to take sole responsibility for the function.

America's relations with the Barbary states were becoming critical, and the arrival of diplomatic dispatches made it necessary for Jefferson and Madison to retire to the President's office for a long meeting. The conference dragged on, so Dolly greeted the guests alone, and by the latter part of the evening she was forced to cope unassisted with those who stayed late. The meeting did not end until long after midnight, when Jefferson went straight to bed.

Madison was so tired he took a nap in one of the guest bedrooms. Dolly continued to entertain Cabinet members, Supreme Court Justices, Senators, Congressmen, and foreign diplomats until dawn. Then, when the last of the visitors had departed, she awakened her husband and took him home. The incident was significant because she handled herself and the situation with brilliant self-confidence, never losing her aplomb. After four years in the limelight under her own roof and that of the President's House, she was charming and gracious, capable of controlling any situation. As she proved conclusively that night, necessity had made her the most accomplished of American hostesses.

A French military attaché, Colonel André de Brionne, who was present at the reception, spoke for many when he said in a letter to Paris that "Mrs. Madison has become one of America's most valuable assets. She would be equally at ease in any of the world's capitals."

Brionne wondered whether Madison appreciated his wife's contributions to the administration, but six months later, after he had become better acquainted with the couple, he formed his own conclusion. "The Secretary of State and his lady," he wrote, "are as inseparable as his duty permits. Never have I known a husband and wife more devoted to each other. Mr. Madison is unstinting in his praise of his lady's virtues, whilst she tells everyone she meets that he is the greatest of living men."

The outbreak of war with the Barbary pirates in April, 1805, put a temporary damper on Washington City social life. Dolly was the first to cancel all of her engagements and to accept no invitations, remarking to Anna that it was "unseemly to be merry when American men at arms are suffering and dying for their country." Within a few months the victory of the United States seemed ensured, however, and by the time the Madisons returned to Washington City after their annual sojourn in Virginia, which was followed by a crisis of their own, they resumed a normal social routine.

It was during this period that politics began to intrude actively in Dolly's life. Her husband was the heir apparent to the Presidency, and Thomas Jefferson was determined that his Secretary of State, intimate friend, and closest collaborator should succeed him. A majority of the Republican-Democratic rank and file appeared to accept the inevitability of the step, but a number of prominent party members began to grumble. Meanwhile the Federalists, realizing that Madison probably would be the man to beat in the election of 1808 made him the principal object of their anti-administration propaganda.

Strong feelings, which cut across party lines, were evident in New York, where Jefferson and Madison had outsmarted themselves by making George Clinton the President's running mate. Vice President Clinton was the most popular man in his home state. A War of Independence general and hero, he was so highly regarded by his fellow citizens that they had accorded him an honor never achieved by any other American, electing him simultaneously to the posts of governor and lieutenant governor.

But Clinton was now sixty-six years of age and would be on the threshold of his seventieth birthday at the time of the next Presidential election, which would thereby virtually eliminate him from consideration for the nation's highest office. His fellow New Yorkers felt, with considerable justice, that Jefferson and Madison had taken deliberate advantage of the state's favorite son, making him Vice President so he would offer the Secretary of State no competition in the next election.

New England, the stronghold of the Federalists, was far stronger in its anti-Madison sentiments. The region was opposed to Jefferson's political philosophy and resented his image of the United States as an agricultural nation. The New England states, particularly Massachusetts, Rhode Island, and Connecticut, were rapidly becoming industrialized, and the economic interests of the region were harmed by administration policies. Year by year the rumblings of discontent grew louder, and they would culminate in an active secession movement that would plague Madison before and during the War of 1812.

The Federalists were the first to strike. A semiliterate public found it difficult to understand disputes over economic and foreign-policy matters, so the most effective attacks were personal. Most American newspapers had not yet adopted self-governing codes of ethics, and no libel laws as yet inhibited the imaginations of editors eager to further the cause of their own party. A majority of newspapers, more numerous in New England than in any other part of the country, had just been founded in recent years and were discovering that scandal-mongering assaults on prominent persons produced the most effective circulation-building results.

The Payne sisters, probably the two best-known women in America, became the immediate, natural targets of the Federalist press. Dolly Madison and Anna Cutts were beautiful, charming, and vivacious, always busy and always in the limelight. Soon after the beginning of Jefferson's second term they became the objects of a smear campaign, actually directed at Secretary Madison through them, that became increasingly virulent as the months passed.

In reality, of course, both were virtuous, straitlaced women who loved their husbands and who led morally impeccable lives. So it was impossible for the editors to name specific partners in their supposed indiscretions. Facts, however, did not inhibit the newspapers, which conducted a campaign of innuendo in which it was charged that Dolly and Anna provided services other than social when they visited the President's House; that the sisters engaged in affairs with foreign diplomats in order to win advantages for Secretary Madison in his dealings with other governments; that Dolly engaged in affairs with Republican-Democratic leaders who could deliver their state's Electoral College votes to Madison in 1808; that Anna, with Dolly's approval, had been having an affair of long standing with her brother-in-law. This sorry matter, the rumors said, had just come to the attention of Congressman Cutts, who was trying in vain to put an end to the relationship. But he was promised a Cabinet position if and when Madison was elected President, so he was tempted to blind himself to his wife's extramarital activities.

Literally nothing in the correspondence of either James or Dolly Madison indicates that they took any notice of the smear campaign. Everyone in a high government position was forced to endure such attacks, and the Madisons appear to have shrugged off the slurs. Federalist members of the Senate and House of Representatives knew the claims were false, were embarrassed by them, and did not hesitate to accept the hospitality of the Madisons. So no harm was done by the slanders.

Congressman Cutts, however, did not display a similar equanimity. Married for only a short time and less accustomed than the Madisons to such attacks, he lost his temper. Perhaps his attitude was influenced, too, by his own precarious position as a Republican-Democrat from a predominantly Federalist state.

He was particularly incensed by the innuendos printed in a new Boston newspaper, the *Federalist*, and wrote a strong letter of protest, in which he challenged the editor to a duel. The killing of Alexander Hamilton by Aaron Burr had resulted in a strong national feeling against dueling, but Cutts was too incensed to care, even though he should have realized that by paying attention to the stories he was giving them validity.

The *Federalist* ignored the letter, although Cutts had dared the editor to print it. The outraged Congressman had sent copies to the more substantial Boston newspapers, but they were reluctant to become involved in the feud and wisely sidestepped the issue.

Suddenly the controversy died away without a duel or other fireworks. The *Federalist*, which had been struggling for existence, went bankrupt, and Cutts was content to take no action.

The smear campaign did assume more serious proportions when some of its claims were accepted by a man of considerable standing. Congressman John Randolph of Roanoke was a colorful maverick, an iconoclast, and a fierce individualist who refused to swear political allegiance to any party. An orator of dubious capabilities who spoke in a high-pitched monotone, he nevertheless was able to hold the House of Representatives spellbound by virtue of his intellectual prowess and the force of his personality. Certainly he was one of the most influential members of the Congress.

Ever since the beginning of Jefferson's presidency, Randolph had been a partner in an uneasy alliance with the administration, supporting the President and Secretary Madison when he approved of their policies, but attacking them with vigor when he disagreed with them. Early in Jefferson's second term, for reasons of his own that he never explained, he broke completely with the administration.

Difficult though it may be to divine Randolph's motives, there can be no doubt that he disapproved of Madison as the successor to the Presidency. He was a gauche, awkward man, socially ill at ease, but it might be going too far to suggest that he became opposed to Madison because he felt uncomfortable at Dolly's dinner parties and suspected—without real cause or substantiation—that she was secretly laughing at him.

In any event, his favorite candidate for the Presidency was James Monroe, a fact that John Quincy Adams was quick to record and repeat. Minister Monroe enjoyed the advantage of being separated from political squabbles by the Atlantic Ocean, but Randolph tried to draw him closer to the source of controversy by writing to him, "Everything is made a business of bargain and traffic, the ultimate object of which is to raise Mr. Madison to the Presidency. To this the old Republican party will never consent. They are united in your support."

(162)

Monroe was completely loyal to Jefferson, his mentor, and to Madison, his adviser and friend. In addition, he was too sound a politician to be misled by the exaggerated claims of his unwanted supporter. In a reply that demonstrated his diplomatic skills, he told Randolph that there were "older men" who had "higher pretensions" to the Presidency, and he emphasized that he would do nothing to harm his own "ancient friendship" with these unnamed persons.

Randolph remained adamant:

To the great and acknowledged influence of [Madison] we are indebted for that strange amalgam of men and principles which has distinguished some of the late acts of the administration and proved so injurious to it. Many, the most consistent of the old republicans, by whose exertions the present men were brought into power, have beheld with immeasurable disgust the principles for which they had contended. . . . They ascribe to the baleful influence of the Secretary of State that we have been gradually relaxing from our old principles, and relapsing into the system of our predecessors.

In a separate paragraph Randolph gave credence to the Federalist canards about Dolly and Anna:

You, my dear Sir, cannot be ignorant—although of all mankind, you perhaps have the least cause to know it— how deeply the respectability of any character may be impaired by an unfortunate matrimonial connexion—I can pursue this subject no farther. It is at once too delicate and too mortifying.

Whether Randolph believed the lies, accepting them at face value, or was merely pretending because the denigration of Madison served his political purposes is impossible to determine. By referring to the rumors with a delicacy contrary to his customary, booming style he indicated that the latter well might be the case.

James Madison lost no sleep over Randolph's opposition to his unannounced candidacy. For two or three years the eccentric Congressman had been regarded as the Republican-Democratic leader in the House of Representatives, but his split with the administration deprived him of his following. Other party members continued to support Jefferson and Madison, and Randolph was isolated.

The President indicated an awareness of Randolph's mischief-making in a letter he sent to Monroe. A man far less sensitive than Monroe would have understood the warning in Jefferson's observation to the effect that "the great body of your friends here are among the firmest adherents of the administration."

Madison remained cheerful and serene in spite of a sprained ankle, suffered when he stumbled on the stoop of his Washington City house. Dolly was her usual ebullient, unruffled self and said nothing to either friends or acquaintances about the Federalist hate campaign. Whether she discussed the matter in private with her husband and sister is unknown. But the family's show of indifference, broken only by Congressman Cutts' one outburst, makes it unlikely that either the Secretary or his lady was seriously concerned.

Other matters were of far greater importance. America's relations with Great Britain were worsening, thanks in large part to the major campaign being waged by Napoleon to isolate and destroy his most obstinate foe. Britain was fighting for her life. The Royal Navy was ordered to keep the sea lanes open to British merchant traffic at all times, and American rights as a neutral were being ignored. Some London authorities continued to regard the United States as a colonial possession, and, as a result,

American merchantmen often were halted and sometimes seized. The illegal impressment of American seamen by the Royal Navy was an even more exacerbating problem, and Madison, struggling in vain to win recognition for his country's rights, had his hands full.

He was further distracted by Dolly's illness. In the summer, during their stay in Virginia, the appearance of a small, tender lump over one knee had bothered her but had not caused her serious concern. By the time the Madisons returned to Washington City the lump had grown larger, had broken open and now refused to heal. Her discomfort increased. She failed to respond to treatment prescribed by local physicians, and it was finally decided that she should seek help from the aptly named Dr. Philip Syng Physick of Philadelphia, one of the most renowned medical practitioners of the era.

The ailment was debilitating and painful, but Dolly's life was not in danger, and she tried to persuade her husband to permit her to go off to Philadelphia alone. He was needed in Washington City, she said, to deal with the British crisis.

But Madison insisted on escorting her to Philadelphia, and remained with her while Dr. Physick began to treat her leg. Surgery could be avoided, the doctor said. He told the patient he could cure her condition in a month by using caustics. Dolly was in low spirits, however, principally because she could not persuade her husband to return to Washington City. She wrote to Anna:

I feel as if my heart was bursting—no mother, no sister— but fool that I am, here is my beloved husband sitting anxiously by me and who is my unremitting nurse. But you know how delicate he is—I tremble for him. On our way one night he was taken very ill with his old bilious complaint. I thought all was over with me. I could not fly to him and aid him as I used to do. But heaven in

its mercy restored him the next morning, and he would
not pause until he heard my fate from Dr. P.

Each day a courier arrived with dispatches for the
Secretary, who spent hours writing to the President, Cabinet colleagues, and State Department subordinates. Dolly
still urged him to return to his own headquarters, where
his burden would be lighter, but he would not listen to her.
She was ill, she needed him, and no crisis could force him
to leave her side.

The couple moved into a handsome suite of rooms on
Sansom Street suitable for a Secretary of State, and Dolly,
in spite of her ailment, enjoyed a social triumph. While
her husband was busy composing his daily letters, she received a stream of callers who visited her in her bedroom
when they discovered she could not hobble to the parlor.
Among the many who came to see her were old Quaker
friends who had chosen to snub her in the months after
her marriage.

Many of her guests demonstrated abiding affection for
her, which was pleasant, but two Quaker ladies, Nancy
Mifflin and Sally Zane, inadvertently created the opposite
effect when they scolded her for allowing hordes of celeb-
rity seekers to invade her bedchamber. It was on this occasion that she wrote to Anna, "I really felt my ancient terror
of [the Quakers] revive to disagreeable degree."

Dolly responded to treatment far more slowly than Dr.
Physick had anticipated, and he decided that, even though
she was improving, she required further treatment. Never
since assuming office had Madison been out of personal
touch with President Jefferson for such a long period, but
he remained adamant in his refusal to part from her, and
Jefferson completely sympathized with him. Relations with
Britain were becoming critical, and as a consequence the
young nation's ties with France were growing more complex. This made it necessary for the President and his chief

subordinate to write each other long letters every day. Dolly was distressed, claiming she was imposing a burden on them, but both ignored her complaints.

In October, 1805, when Dolly was convalescing and it appeared she soon might be able to return to Washington City, a new epidemic of yellow fever alarmed Philadelphia. Dr. Physick advised that, as his patient had not yet completely recovered her health and the epidemic might spread to other cities, it would be wise to isolate her in the country and minimize her vulnerability.

Secretary Madison promptly took his wife to Gray's Ferry on the Schuylkill River, where he rented a house for a month. They arrived a scant twenty-four hours before other refugees from Philadelphia overflowed the little town, and only because of Madison's position was it possible to hire a household staff.

The international problems facing the President and Cabinet were becoming still more intricate, and Jefferson decided to take no definitive action until Madison could confer with him in person and at length. Dolly's sense of guilt increased, but she failed to move her husband, and she wrote again to Anna Cutts, bewailing the stubborn attitude of her "beloved husband" and her own "indisposition."

By late October the epidemic subsided and Dolly's leg was virtually healed, so Madison took her back to Philadelphia. The cautious Dr. Physick advised that she remain for a time longer, however, saying she might suffer a relapse on the rough, pit-filled roads that led to the nation's capital.

The Secretary of State could delay his own return no longer. A possible war with Spain was threatening, France was unhappy in her relations with the United States, and Great Britain was becoming intransigent. President Jefferson urgently required his presence, and he finally agreed to go back to Washington City.

Never since he and Dolly had been married had they

been separated for more than a single night at a time. Now that the time had come for an unavoidable parting, however, both were filled with dread. Dolly tried to conquer her fears by agreeing that it was wrong to continue to rely exclusively on the help of her elderly mother, who had gone to the Madison home in the capital to look after fifteen-year-old Payne Todd.

Dolly's comments in the daily notes she wrote to her husband amply illustrate the love she bore him. "A few hours only have passed since you left me my beloved," she wrote, "and I find that nothing can relieve the oppression of my mind but speaking to you in this the only way."

The next night she was awakened by a severe thunderstorm, and became alarmed for his safety. "Detention, cold and accident seem to menace thee."

Her own physical condition was continuing to improve, she told him in her next letter, and she forbade him to squander his substance by worrying about her. "Adieu, my beloved, our hearts understand each other," she concluded.

Her relief was infinite when he wrote that he had reached Washington City safely and that he loved her. "To find you love me, have my child safe and that my mother is well," she told him, "seems to comprise all my happiness."

Personal matters were not her sole concern, however, and in each note she inquired anxiously about developments in America's relations with the major powers of Europe. Madison obviously recognized her interest as legitimate and gave her capsule reports, telling her the latest news in the fewest possible words.

Early in November Dolly sent her husband the happy news that she would be given a medical discharge in a few days, adding that "the doctor regards you more than any man he knows."

A delighted Madison returned the compliment. Always

remote and composed in his voluminous political correspondence, never showing emotion, he displayed a different facet of his complex nature in his reply to Dolly. The word that she was coming home at last, he wrote, "gives me much happiness, but it cannot be complete till I have you again with me." He was relieved to learn that Anna and Richard Cutts were stopping in Philadelphia en route from Boston to Washington City and would escort Dolly, as it had worried him that she would be traveling alone. He closed by saying that this was "the last mail, my dearest, that will be likely to find you in Philadelphia and I am not without some hope that this will be too late."

After being forced to rest for so long, Dolly engaged in a whirlwind of activities before returning home. She collected the rent due on the house she owned, and finally heeding the often-repeated advice of her husband, she took out an insurance policy on the property. She bought "a handsome pair" of carriage horses "for a price you will most heartily approve" to replace the team that had been sold prior to her departure for medical treatment. She also attended to some purchases Jefferson had requested as a favor, including a "fashionable wig" for his daughter, Martha Randolph.

In her own final letter she expressed her relief and gratitude that Madison had made arrangements for Payne's future schooling. Her comments were bland, and it is necessary to read between the lines in order to understand their full import.

For all practical purposes the boy regarded Madison as his father and called him "Papa," but the Secretary of State could not give Payne as much paternal attention as he wished. Dolly may have spoiled her only son over the years, although no direct evidence on the subject is available. Be that as it may, Payne Todd was already demonstrating the lack of regard for the feelings of others that would cause his mother problems and heartache in the future.

It was apparent that he needed discipline, and Madison made arrangements with Roman Catholic Bishop John Carroll of Baltimore for Payne's admission to a new school in his diocese that, as a matter of principle, accepted students of every faith. The headmaster was a remarkable priest, Father Louis Dubourg, a West Indian of French descent, who ultimately became an archbishop. Father Dubourg, who knew how to handle boys and tolerated no nonsense from his pupils, agreed to accept Payne.

It was typical of Madison that he was pleased because French was included in the curriculum of St. Mary's College. He had taught himself to read French fluently and could understand it well enough in conversation, but he couldn't speak a word and required the services of an interpreter when dealing with some French diplomats. Payne, he was delighted to report, would acquire talents that he himself lacked.

For feminine reasons of her own Dolly had soured on the French and their civilization. Late in 1804 Napoleon had sent a new minister to the United States, General Louis-Marie Turreau, a bald, red-faced hero of the French Revolution who sported a large moustache. Turreau boasted of his ferocity toward his enemies and was so crude that he succeeded in offending the Washington ladies, none more than Dolly.

What really infuriated her was his attitude toward his own wife, a tiny, delicate woman with a temper that matched his. They quarreled frequently, and it was common knowledge that the exasperated Turreau often struck her. On one occasion, according to Senator Plumer, he beat her with a walking stick. Violent jealousy was one of Turreau's many faults, and he habitually locked his wife in their house whenever he absented himself from

Washington City. Neighbors who took pity on the lady made it their business to release her on these occasions, thereby earning her husband's anger.

No one felt greater contempt for Turreau than Dolly Madison, but she was not in a position to express her feelings freely. As the wife of the Secretary of State, she could not snub the minister without risking the ire of the thin-skinned Napoleon, who regarded his diplomatic representatives as mere extensions of his own person.

For months prior to her departure from the capital, Dolly had been rigidly polite to Turreau, inviting him to dinners and receptions when necessary, but treating him with an impersonal chill that made her own feelings clear to everyone who knew her. Her husband and President Jefferson didn't want to offend the Emperor of the French at a time when America's relations with Great Britain and Spain were growing increasingly precarious, but Dolly refused to relax her stand against the man she privately called "the butcher" and "the fighting husband."

The night before her departure for Washington City she gave a reception for her old Philadelphia friends, and Turreau, who was paying a visit to the city, decided to attend, even though he had not been invited. He succeeded in ruining the evening for his infuriated hostess and her uncomfortable guests by drinking to excess, delivering long monologues in a loud voice, and otherwise behaving like a boor.

Anna Cutts, who had arrived with her husband to escort Dolly back to Washington City, described the party in a letter to old Mrs. Payne and made a significant observation. Only Dolly's "great love for Mr. Madison," she said, deterred her from creating an international incident by ordering Turreau to leave.

XVI

$\mathcal{D}$olly was able to put the unpleasant encounter with General Turreau out of her mind when she and her husband were reunited. They had been separated for almost six weeks, but now she was content. Senator Plumer, who saw her a few days after her return, wrote that she was "as radiant as any bride."

The visits of unusual official guests made the 1805–1806 Washington City social season unique, but Dolly was experienced enough to cope. The first to arrive was Ambassador Sidi Suliman Mellimelli, a Turk who came as the envoy of the Bey of Tunis. A gray-bearded man of about fifty, he arrived with a retinue of eleven, including his pipe bearer and three musicians. As a special gift he brought four blooded Arabian horses, which Jefferson accepted in the name of the American people.

The United States government was responsible for the full support of the envoy, and Secretary Madison had his hands full. He rented the boardinghouse of a man named Stelle and arranged for the proprietor to provide meals for the Tunisian party. Mellimelli was eminently satisfied with the arrangements, but complained privately to Madison that he required the services of a concubine. The Secretary engaged one "Georgia, a Greek," charging her fee to the State Department with the notation, written in the account book in his own hand, "Appropriations to foreign intercourse are terms of great latitude and may be drawn on by very urgent and unforeseen occurrences."

The expenses of Mellimelli's visit were great, but farmers Jefferson and Madison consoled themselves with the thought that, in the long run, the ambassador's visit would be profitable. They would charge a substantial fee, they decided, for mating the handsome Arabian gift stallion with local mares.

Dolly Madison entertained Mellimelli under her own roof and at the President's House, showing him every courtesy and inviting everyone of importance in the capital to meet him. It must be presumed that the Secretary of State, who understood his wife, refrained from telling her about the hiring of Georgia the Greek. Had Dolly known, she would have refused to receive the ambassador, and the good ladies of Washington City would have rallied to her cause, forcing Jefferson and Madison to entertain Mellimelli only at stag dinners.

In November delegations of American Indians representing the nations of the West began to arrive in Washington City for talks with the President and Secretary of State. Both sides hoped to negotiate treaties in which the rights of both sides would be recognized. The first to arrive were the Creeks, who were soon followed by the Osage, Missouri, Mississippi, Sac, Sioux, and Pawnee. The last to appear were chiefs of the powerful Cherokee. The Osage had the largest delegation, sending twenty-one representatives, but the exact number of Indians who came to Washington City is a matter in some dispute, even within the Madison family. The Secretary's official list contained eighty-three names; his wife's social register listed ninety-one.

To the astonishment of Eastern Seaboard dwellers and foreigners who knew nothing about Indians, the represen-

(173)

tatives of the various tribes were very different. Some wore blue tailcoats, while others, in spite of the cold, appeared naked to the waist, their torsos smeared with paint. Some sported hats trimmed in gold, while others wore feathers in their scalp locks. A number had been educated in settlers' schools and spoke a perfect, unaccented English, but some could converse only in their own tongues and required the services of interpreters. Some sat at a dinner table, using silverware with ease, but the representatives of several groups preferred to squat on the floor and eat with their hands.

Dolly displayed her customary, enthusiastic aplomb, giving a number of dinner parties and receptions at which the guest list included Senators, Supreme Court justices, Indian delegations, and Ambassador Mellimelli. Almost everyone of consequence in the city came to the Madison house on New Year's Day, 1806, where several guests saw the somewhat pompous Senator John Quincy Adams of Massachusetts, the turbaned Mellimelli, and a half-naked Sioux chief immersed in a discussion of theology.

Merry, the British envoy, again felt insulted, this time because he believed the Indians were receiving attention that should have been devoted to him, the senior diplomat present. He left after a token visit, but there were no other casualties.

The secret of Dolly Madison's success was best illustrated, perhaps, by her conduct at this affair. Nothing upset her, and she devoted time and consideration to every guest, regardless of nationality or position. She showed the same courtesy to an illiterate savage that she gave to the Spanish minister. She was undisturbed when one of the Osage tore a chunk of meat apart with his hands and crammed it into his mouth. She made it her business to chat with each of the Indians, and she made certain that Ambassador Mellimelli was served no dish that might offend his Muslim sensibilities.

Only in her response to General Turreau of France did she draw an invisible line, and she was applauded by every woman at the party. Madame Turreau received her special attention, and Dolly presented some of the Indians to her, but she allowed the French minister to fend for himself after doing her minimal duty as a hostess by making certain he had been served cold meats, cake, and a spiced rum punch so potent that Secretary Madison was afraid some of the Indians might become intoxicated and disgrace themselves.

Mellimelli's visit had a tragicomic ending. President Jefferson and Secretary Madison flatly refused to pay the tribute demanded of the United States by the Bey of Tunis. Mellimelli started for home by way of New York, intending to sail from Boston, but was enjoying his stay in the United States so much that, in the early summer of 1806, he announced his intention of visiting Monticello and Montpelier.

The alarmed Jefferson and Madison took frantic measures to speed Mellimelli on his way, but three members of his party—his secretary, his cook, and his barber—were inadvertently stranded. Madison arranged their passage to England, and the British government ultimately sent the Secretary of State a bill for their lodging in London. He refused to pay it, and a new diplomatic quarrel broke out, although it was forgotten when larger issues loomed. Nothing in the State Department records indicates the ultimate fate of the unfortunate Turkish trio.

In 1806, as Jefferson neared the halfway point in his second term, the Administration had far more to worry about than the treatment of eccentric visitors to the capital. Critics of the Republican-Democrats, led by John Randolph, were becoming more vociferous, and Madison shared the President's concern, even though the gadfly attacks failed to hamper the passage of legislation the administration wanted.

A rumor began to circulate in the spring to the effect that the Federalists, meeting in informal caucus, had voted in favor of establishing and maintaining a social boycott of their opponents. No announcement would be made, but party members would refuse to attend any function given by the President or members of his Cabinet.

Always small town in its flavor from the time of its founding, Washington City could keep no secrets. Word of the unofficial boycott leaked out in a few days, and soon was called to the attention of Jefferson and Madison, who deplored the introduction of a vindictive element into the fabric of capital society.

Dolly laughed when her husband told her the Federalists' intentions, and both Madison and Jefferson became even more upset when she refused to accept the threat at face value. Democracy, they argued, was still a fragile institution and might lack the strength to survive a series of personal vendettas.

But Dolly solved the problem in her own way. She planned a number of dinner parties, extending invitations to most Senators and Congressmen, regardless of their party affiliations. They responded precisely as she anticipated, happily accepting. She was right in assuming that no responsible American politician would reject an invitation to dine at the home of the Secretary of State. Thus the boycott was terminated before it could begin.

Not until much later did it dawn on such admiring observers as Margaret Bayard Smith that Dolly had stacked the cards in her own favor by refraining from inviting Randolph and a few other hotheads who might have refused and consequently upset her balanced calculations.

The Madisons lived in an era when, in effect, Washington City was one big club, and everyone of consequence was familiar with everyone else. As a result, most political attacks acquired a personal coloration, and those who opposed each other in principle soon became involved in bitter feuds that stopped ordinarily sensible men from speaking to each other.

James Madison never descended to the personal level throughout his long public career, and unlike the great majority of his contemporaries, he took no offense when he was attacked. Such assaults were an integral part of the political game, so he discounted them in advance. He taught Dolly the same approach from the time of their marriage, and she developed an impenetrable armor, too.

The imperturbability of the Madisons is exemplified by the attitude they displayed in June, 1806, when John Randolph launched a vitriolic attack on the Secretary of State in a Congressional speech that quickly became the talk of the town.

Late that same day the Madisons paid a visit to the country house of the Samuel Harrison Smiths, and Mrs. Smith marveled at their equanimity. "Mr. M," she wrote, "was in one of his most sportive moods, and Mrs. M was all that was tender, affectionate and attractive, as usual."

When Dolly wished, she could depersonalize any relationship. Throughout the better part of 1806 Secretary Madison heard unverifiable rumors that former Vice President Aaron Burr was trying to establish an empire of his own in the West and was seeking contributions of men, money, and munitions from Great Britain and Spain. In March, 1807, the adventurer was captured and sent to Richmond for trial before Chief Justice John Marshall. Evidence of Burr's guilt was lacking, and the sly New Yorker was acquitted, but his reputation was in such shreds that he had no choice but to flee to Europe, where he lived in great want and disgrace.

Burr's spectacular career became the capital's principal topic of conversation, but Dolly refused to reveal her

(177)

personal feelings in the matter, if she had any, even to those closest to her. Writing to Anna, who was out of town at the time, about her former would-be suitor, she confined herself to a dry recital of facts. "I suppose you have heard that Colonel Burr is retaken and on his way to Richmond for trial. That is all I know."

In June, 1807, the Madisons left Washington City for their annual visit to Montpelier. They were delayed en route by torrential rains. Dolly wrote that "my limbs yet tremble with the terrors and fatigue of our journey," and soon after her arrival she fell ill again, this time suffering from excruciatingly painful inflammatory rheumatism. Madison's mother nursed her, as did his niece, Nelly, who was now married to a physician, Dr. John Willis.

She became the patient of Dr. Willis, who did what he could by prescribing medication and bleeding her, but he was frank to admit that only rest could alleviate her condition. She was forced to remain in bed during a visit that brought twenty-five members of the Madison clan to Montpelier. But she insisted on taking her place at the table when President Jefferson stopped off for dinner on his way to Monticello.

By July she had regained sufficient strength to resume her normal activities, and late in the month a horde of Paynes descended on Montpelier. The family reunion became a celebration when it was learned that Anna Cutts had just given birth to her third child.

The Madisons exchanged a number of visits with Jefferson throughout the summer, continuing a custom of many years' standing. But they did not go to the nearby home of the James Monroes, who had recently come home from Europe, nor did the recently retired diplomat visit them.

Ostensibly retaining a surface friendship, Madison and Monroe were drifting apart. Contrary to the wishes of Jefferson, Monroe had succumbed to the pressures of John

Randolph and was lending a receptive ear to those who wanted to advance his candidacy for the nation's highest office. Dolly and her husband took it virtually for granted that Madison would become his party's candidate and were somewhat shaken by Monroe's lack of loyalty.

Dolly considered Elizabeth Monroe responsible and wrote privately to Anna that she had never liked or trusted the woman. It must be assumed that she communicated these same views to her husband, and that they made sense to him.

Urgent matters of State occupied Jefferson and his Secretary that summer. British attacks on American merchant shipping had become intolerable, and Madison had instituted a campaign to establish an import embargo on British manufactured goods and on the export of American raw materials to Britain. The Federalists of New England defied the embargo, however, their section of the country being economically dependent upon Anglo-American trade. So the embittered Madison knew his policy was a failure, and he worked strenuously but in vain to find some other way to protect American commerce.

Dolly took no active part in these matters, but her husband kept her informed of developments. She admired him so much that her attitude was simple: Whatever he believed was right.

By the time the Madisons returned to Washington City in the autumn of 1807, politics was in the air. Jefferson and his principal subordinate had achieved a complete understanding, and the President repeatedly told visitors that he expected his Secretary of State to succeed him. The Republican-Democratic rank and file in most parts of the country agreed, and members of the foreign diplomatic corps began to treat both Madison and Dolly with a new deference.

The Federalists, who were popular only in New England, lacked the strength to win the election. This meant that anyone with Presidential ambitions would be forced to defeat Madison inside his own party. Several rebel groups were ready to try.

The embargo against Great Britain had antagonized the Republican-Democrats of New England, and they joined forces with dissidents in New York, New Jersey, and Pennsylvania who believed the Presidency should go to someone other than a Virginian, two of the three holders of the office having come from that state.

These rebels were unwilling to back the candidacy of James Monroe, but John Randolph and his friends would not yield. The New Englanders and the men from the Middle Atlantic states finally settled on Vice President Clinton who, in spite of his age, appeared to be the only man of stature available.

Caucuses were held on both national and state levels, beginning in January, 1808. The most important was the caucus in Washington City of Republican-Democratic Senators and Congressmen. Of the eighty-nine present, eighty-three cast their ballots for Madison. A total of seventy-nine endorsed Clinton for Vice President. But the New England and Middle Atlantic dissidents insisted upon nominating Clinton separately for the Presidency, so he was placed in the curious position of being a candidate for both of the nation's highest offices.

The Monroe forces worked energetically, but even in Virginia and the Carolinas they could not muster much enthusiasm for their candidate, and the pro-Madison party regulars rallied there, making it obvious that Monroe could not win.

James Monroe was a sensible man and a sound politician, so in the spring of 1808 he not only withdrew from the race but announced that he was giving his unqualified support to his old friend and neighbor, James Madison. Late in the spring he made a trip to Washington City, and an equally practical Madison agreed to

(180)

bury the hatchet. Able men would be needed in the new administration, and it seemed only natural that the experienced Monroe, who had a following of his own, would be offered a place in the Cabinet. President Jefferson, soon to become an elder statesman, approved of the peace pact.

Dolly entertained Monroe at dinner during his stay in the capital and, like her husband, displayed no animosity toward him. Elizabeth Monroe stayed in Virginia because she was suffering from an "indisposition," but it is impossible to determine whether her ailment was real or diplomatic. Certainly Dolly Madison, by now the most polished hostess in the brief history of the United States, would have extended a dinner invitation to Mrs. Monroe as well as her husband. It is possible, however, that Elizabeth—her own hope of becoming First Lady dashed—was not yet ready to face the cool appraisal of her successful rival. James Monroe's future would depend in large part on the post the next President would offer him, and the Monroes were not anxious to run the risk of further antagonizing the next President's wife.

The Federalists, hoping for a miracle but knowing none would save them, persuaded Charles C. Pinckney of South Carolina to become their candidate for President. Then they nominated Rufus King of New York for the Vice Presidency.

Dolly paid virtually no attention to the maneuvers that ensured her husband's election as President. A personal tragedy, striking unexpectedly, drove everything else from her mind and heart. She received word that her beloved mother had died suddenly of a stroke.

Retiring to the privacy of her own suite, Dolly made no more public appearances in Washington City, and two dinner parties she had scheduled were canceled. She remained with her husband, to be sure, and accompanied him to Montpelier for the summer, as usual, but her stay there was quiet, and she did not resume her normal social life until the autumn.

Madison needed no special help from his wife in the summer of 1808 for the simple reason that he did not bother to campaign actively for the Presidency. Unlike Vice President Clinton, who toured the country on his own behalf and made addresses everywhere he could drum up an audience, Madison did not make a single campaign speech. He issued no campaign statements, and he made it plain to the American people that his duties as Secretary of State fully occupied his time.

He also discouraged political visitors and office seekers, who would have besieged Montpelier had he opened the doors to them. He was making no deals with anyone, he wrote to John Quincy Adams, who had become his firm foreign-affairs supporter and consequently had won the enmity of the Federalists. He intended to enter the office of President beholden to no man.

It has been taken for granted, however, that Madison and Thomas Jefferson discussed the composition of the next Cabinet during the course of their frequent summer conferences at Monticello and Montpelier. The weary Jefferson had no intention of interfering in the affairs of the next administration, but Madison had been seeking his counsel for many years, and it is unlikely that he would have turned away from his mentor and close friend at this stage of his career.

By the beginning of October the Madisons were back in their F Street House, and the following month balloting began. The official results were announced on December 7, and to the surprise of no one, Madison received 122 Electoral College votes to 47 for Pinckney and 6 for Clinton, who was reelected Vice President. Madison's victory was emphatic in Vermont, Pennsylvania, New Jersey, Virginia, South and North Carolina, Georgia, Kentucky, Tennessee, and Ohio. He also won New York in a hotly contested election. Pinckney came out ahead only in New Hampshire, Massachusetts, Connecticut, Rhode Island, and Delaware.

In the three months remaining before he took office, Madison continued to serve as Secretary of State. His position was uncomfortable because he still represented Thomas Jefferson, but at the same time the chiefs of foreign legations listened to him as though he were already President.

Dolly was similarly treated by diplomats' wives and the wives and daughters of office seekers. Acting on her initiative, she and her husband scheduled no social engagements for the period prior to the inauguration and accepted invitations only from old friends. A frequent guest was Representative John G. Jackson of Virginia, a staunch Madison supporter and Dolly's brother-in-law; his wife, the former Mary Payne, had died the previous year, as had all but one of their children, and he regarded the Madisons as his only living family.

Madison juggled his two hats with the dexterity of a man long accustomed to diplomacy. In his State Department office he conducted the nation's foreign affairs and would discuss politics with no one. At home he became the President-elect and conferred nightly with Republican-Democratic office holders and other party leaders. He also made it his business to consult with Federalist Senators and Congressmen.

Dolly, equally experienced, was conspicuous by her absence. Bread, cheese, and cold meats were available in the dining room, and pitchers of ale stood on a sideboard. But the hostess appeared only when her husband's guests stayed too late. Then, determined to guard his health, which she always regarded as delicate, she came to the door, bed lamp in hand. Even the most insensitive visitors took the hint.

Dolly played no part in the formation of the Cabinet,

and it is not known whether Madison even discussed the composition of his office family with her in private. She knew, naturally, that it would be her duty to maintain friendly relations with Cabinet wives and daughters.

Two key posts went to holdovers from the Jefferson Administration. Madison admired the talented Albert Gallatin, with whom he had worked in harmony for eight years, and, in fact, wanted Gallatin to take the State Department. But the Secretary of the Treasury preferred to remain in his old place, and when Jefferson supported his stand, Madison agreed. The competent Attorney General, Caesar Rodney of Delaware, also was pleased to accept Madison's offer to remain in office.

Posterity has been critical of Madison's appointments to the War and Navy Departments, which were of little importance in times of peace, but required chiefs of strength, wisdom, and determination when war with Great Britain seemed increasingly inevitable. Dr. William Eustis, the distinguished New England physician who became Secretary of War, had no qualfications for his post other than his devotion to the Republican-Democratic party. In order to give the Cabinet a balanced regional representation, Madison made Paul Hamilton of South Carolina his Secretary of the Navy. He, too, was a party stalwart, but had no other characteristics of note.

Senator Samuel Smith of Maryland, strongly supported by a number of influential colleagues, urged Madison to give the State Department to his brother, Robert, the outgoing Secretary of the Navy. The President-elect hesitated. State was the most important position in the Cabinet, and since both he and Jefferson had served there, it was rightly regarded as a stepping-stone to the Presidency. Madison had sat in the Cabinet with Robert Smith for eight long years and suffered no illusions about him, knowing him to be charming, vain, weak, and inefficient.

His appointment would make it necessary for the incoming President to act as his own Secretary of State, for all practical purposes, and it was for this very reason that Madison finally gave the post to Smith. Foreign affairs would be of paramount importance in the years ahead, and Madison wanted his own hand at the helm.

While Madison wrestled with his problems, Dolly was busy making extensive plans of her own. After living in Washington City for the past eight years she understood the town well, and knew what was necessary to accomplish her ends. She took no one but Anna into her confidence and waited until she actually became First Lady before she revealed her thoughts to others.

XVII

*O*n March 4, 1809, the weather was warm, with more than a hint of spring in the air. Army and Navy bands played lively airs, and huge crowds gathered early on Pennsylvania Avenue and the Capitol lawns, many people having come from Baltimore and other cities for the inauguration.

A half hour before the start of the ceremonies Dolly Madison left her F Street house and was accompanied in her carriage by Congressman and Mrs. Cutts. She wore a gorgeous bonnet of purple velvet trimmed in white satin, topped by two huge, white plumes, and her gown was concealed by a long cloak of white wool, edged in purple.

Seats had been reserved for her in the gallery of the House of Representatives, a similar honor having been given only to members of the diplomatic corps and justices of the Supreme Court. This was a democratic festival, and at the specific request of the President-elect, all other seats had been made available to the general public, so all the places were taken.

Senators and Congressmen filled the main floor of the hall, and when Thomas Jefferson came up the center aisle alone a few minutes before noon, he was accorded a standing ovation. He was wearing an ill-fitting suit of rusty black, and he looked weary.

Two battalions of cavalry escorted James Madison

to the Capitol, and he entered the hall with Secretaries Smith and Gallatin, Attorney General Rodney, and Jefferson's private secretary, Isaac Coles. A reception committee of Senators and Congressmen escorted him to the podium.

The oath of office was administered by Chief Justice of the United States John Marshall, who must have been unhappy, because he had privately opposed Madison's election. It was noted that the new Chief Executive's suit resembled Jefferson's, which was no coincidence. In a joint attempt to encourage American manufacturers, they had been cut from the same bolt of Connecticut cloth and fashioned by the same tailor.

The fourth President of the United States bowed to his predecessor and the Chief Justice, smiled at his wife, and delivered a brief, mundane inauguration address in which he revealed none of the policy changes—if any—that he planned to make. Leaving the hall, he waited for Dolly on the Capitol steps as cannon roared a salute to him and the troops that lined both sides of Pennsylvania Avenue held back the crowds.

Jefferson, who found it increasingly difficult to organize his private life, had not yet vacated the White House, which the newspapers called by that name for the first time in their stories about the occasion. Therefore, the reception was held in the F Street house, which was crammed with more people than it could hold. Margaret Bayard Smith wrote in her diary that she had to wait in line for a half hour before being admitted.

She found the new President and First Lady in a cramped corner of the drawing room, where they were accepting the congratulations of their too-numerous guests. Dolly "looked extremely beautiful, was drest in a plain cambrick-dress with a very long train, plain around the neck without any handkerchief. . . . She was all dignity, grace and affability."

(187)

The last well-wishers left the house late in the afternoon, and the tired Madisons ate a light meal. Then, while the President went to bed for an hour, Dolly changed into a pale, buff-colored velvet dress. It, too, featured a daringly low neckline, which she emphasized with a string of pearls. She wore her purple bonnet again when she and her husband went to a gala ball at Long's Hotel, which had been leased for the occasion.

Jefferson arrived at the hotel shortly before the Madisons appeared. He was in high spirits, and remarked that this was a far happier occasion for him that for his successor. He was now a "plain, unassuming citizen," he said, and the thought pleased him.

The orchestra played *"Madison's March,"* which had been composed for the occasion, and Dolly was escorted into the ballroom by one of the affair's organizers. According to an enraptured Mrs. Smith, she "looked a queen," and her manners "would disarm envy itself, and conciliate even enemies." It may have been anticlimactic when the President appeared, with Anna Cutts on his arm.

Care was taken not to offend the foreign diplomats, and French Minister Turreau escorted Dolly to the supper table. Nothing in her attitude indicated her private opinion of him. They were followed by Anna and British Minister David Erskine. Madison came next with Mrs. Robert Smith, who was annoyed because, even though the President was her escort, Anna had been given precedence over her.

In many ways the early nineteenth century resembled later periods in American history. Only the powerful, the renowned, and the wealthy attended the ball, but the public was allowed to watch from the balcony. A huge crowd gathered, and the organizers of the affair were unable to exercise control. Uninvited guests by the hundreds drifted down to the main hall.

Dolly was the center of interest, and few paid any attention to those noted Fathers of their Country, the third and fourth Presidents of the United States. The First Lady was applauded every time she took a bite of food, sipped her wine, or made a remark to someone. She thought it would be a gracious gesture to visit each table to thank other guests for their attendance, but so many people surrounded her that she narrowly escaped injury and had to abandon the idea.

Jefferson enjoyed the party, spending his time beaming first at Madison, then at Dolly. Margaret Bayard Smith, who never missed a nuance, observed that "a father never loved a son more than he loves Mr. Madison."

Dolly had the time of her life. This was her night of triumph, and she savored every moment as she laughed and chatted. Her husband was exhausted, however, and by the middle of the evening wondered aloud how soon he could go to bed.

The crowd became still heavier as the party progressed, and the heat in the ballroom became unbearable. Eventually several energetic young men broke the upper panes of glass in the windows in order to improve the ventilation, but they managed only to chill parts of the room.

Former President Jefferson danced with Dolly, then took his leave, and a score of prominent gentlemen claimed the right to lead the lovely First Lady to the dance floor. The President looked repeatedly at his watch, yawned, and feebly tried to tease the ladies who sat near him. By ten o'clock he could tolerate no more, and Dolly, who had been watching him covertly, took his arm and led him to their carriage two hours before the party ended.

Newspapers throughout the United States were enthusiastic in their approval of Dolly, and only the most reactionary element of the Federalist press failed to express admiration for the President's sterling qualities. A rare exception was Mrs. Frances Few, Gallatin's sister-in-law, who was present at all of the inaugural festivities and who failed to appreciate either Madison's steady calm or his wife's exuberance. Obviously but privately disapproving, Mrs. Few wrote:

Mr. Madison . . . is a small man quite devoid of dignity in his appearance—he bows very low and never looks at the person to whom he is bowing but keeps his eyes on the ground. His skin looks like parchment—at first I thought this appearance was occasioned by the smallpox but upon a nearer approach I found this was not the case—a few moments in his company and you lose sight of these defects and will see nothing but what pleases you —his eyes are penetrating and expressive—his smile charming—his manners affable—his conversation lively and interesting.

Mrs. Madison is a handsome woman—looks much younger that her husband—she is tall and majestic—her manners affable but a little affected. She has been very much admired and is still fond of admiration—loads herself with finery and dresses without any taste—and amidst all her finery you may discover that in neatness she is very deficient. Her complexion is brilliant—her neck and bosom the most beautiful I ever saw—her face expresses nothing but good nature. It is impossible to be with her . . . and not be pleased. There is something very fascinating about her—yet I do not think it possible to know what her real opinions are. She is all things to all men—not the least of a prude as she one day told an old bachelor and held up her mouth for him to kiss.

Dolly's legions of admirers were far less critical, and in their opinion she could do no wrong. She seemed to take on a larger-than-life quality, attributed in monarchies to royalty, and almost two centuries later to motion picture stars. Crowds followed her whenever she appeared in public, and she seemed to mesmerize those who met her for the first time.

Thomas Jefferson needed a full week after the inception of the new administration to collect his huge library, his inventions, his incredibly voluminous correspondence, his piles of documents, his stacks of newspaper clippings on subjects that interested him, and, of course, his few items of threadbare clothing. He left the White House on March 11, and the following day the Madisons moved in, taking up residence in a suite on the southwest corner. Congressman Richard Cutts and Anna Payne, with their three sons, moved in too, and in the next six years would be joined by two daughters. A room was set aside for Payne Todd, who was still attending school in Baltimore. The only other permanent resident at this time was Edward Coles, Dolly's cousin, who had been engaged as the President's private secretary.

Various numbers of the Madison and Payne families were frequent visitors, and John Quincy Adams commented that one of the President's young nephews or nieces was always underfoot. In 1810 Lucy Payne Washington became a widow and moved in with her sister and brother-in-law, bringing her three sons with her. She remained at the White House until 1812, when she became the wife of Associate Justice Thomas Todd of the Supreme Court.

Immediately after becoming the mistress of the President's mansion Dolly unveiled her plan. She took key Senators and Representatives on tours of the place, and they could see for themselves that, in the eight years it had been occupied by a widower indifferent to his physical surroundings, it had become rundown and shabby.

It was the members of Congress, not Dolly, who said the official residence of the President was a national disgrace and needed an immediate face lifting. They promised to provide the necessary funds without delay, and they kept their word. One of the first bills passed by the Congress after Madison's inauguration appropriated for the purpose what was then a very large sum, $26,000. Of this, $14,000 was to be spent for decorations, furnishings, and landscaping, and $12,000 for building improvements and repairs. The entire project was to be supervised by Benjamin H. Latrobe, one of the most noted architects of the period, who enjoyed the trust of the Congress.

Latrobe was no match for Dolly and soon became the instrument of her will. They quarreled frequently and enthusiastically, and Dolly won every argument, thereby placing the mark of her taste on the White House, an influence that other First Ladies accepted and that, as a consequence, has persisted down to the present day.

A number of new public and private rooms were added, the central staircase was enlarged, and indoor plumbing was installed in the President's living quarters. Dolly insisted on papering the main drawing room in a yellow satin, made available by Napoleon's Paris decorator, and herself purchased red velvet for draperies. Latrobe was horrified, saying the garish colors lacked dignity, but Dolly's will prevailed and he backed down, eventually conceding that she had been right.

The previous year she had seen and admired a handsome blond piano in the French legation, so one that was almost identical was ordered from Paris, and the White House acquired its first permanent musical instrument. Dolly selected the patterns for china and silverware, refused to permit the installation of several ornamental mirrors purchased by Latrobe until she inspected them, and not even andirons were put into place until she approved them. For her husband's convenience she also put in a new, expanded wine cellar.

In matters relating to the new lawns and gardens that would replace a wilderness tangle outside the White

House Dolly deferred to the President, saying he was the expert. So Madison approved the landscaping plans and himself directed the emplacements of trees, bushes, and ornamental shrubs.

Dolly enjoyed a stroke of good fortune when she was able to hire the most accomplished chef in Washington City, John Sioussa, who had been in the employ of the recalled British minister, Anthony Merry. Sioussa not only made a vast improvement in the menus, but gave the White House table a dignity it had lacked.

By the end of May the refurnishing had progressed sufficiently for Dolly to hold the first of her "Wednesday drawing rooms," social occasions that would acquire international renown and make secure her own place as the leading hostess of the period. These receptions were held throughout both of Madison's terms, and were suspended only during the most harrowing days of the War of 1812.

Each week as many as fifty to one hundred ladies and gentlemen were present, and Margaret Bayard Smith said that no wife ever rejected an invitation. Among those present were Cabinet members and Supreme Court justices, Senators and Congressmen, foreign diplomats and any distinguished visitors who happened to be in town. Parents connived and schemed in order to obtain invitations for their eligible daughters, and many years later Dolly remarked that she knew of "two score" of married couples who had met at her receptions.

A military band stationed behind screens played light airs as guests entered and went through the receiving line, where Dolly sometimes was joined by a prominent visitor. Cookies, cakes, ice cream, and fresh fruit were piled on buffet tables, and a nonalcoholic punch was served.

The Wednesday drawing rooms began promptly at three P.M., and guests were ushered out precisely two hours later. Dolly was the star attraction, and a crowd invariably gathered around her, eager to repeat any observations or witty comment she might make. She enjoyed the receptions immensely.

More often than not, the President made an appearance, arriving late and leaving early. Only pressing business kept him away. Madison hated large, formal gatherings, and it was obvious that he was late because he loathed standing in a receiving line. It also embarrassed him when everyone present stood as he entered the room. He was so ill at ease and often so bored that Washingtonians rightly concluded he was making a sacrifice for his wife's sake, accepting her concept of the enhancement of the dignity surrounding the Presidency.

As the White House years passed Madison became increasingly adept in finding ways to alleviate his distress at Dolly's drawing rooms. Looking strangely old-fashioned in his black suit and powdered wig, he retired to a far corner with a Senator, the head of a foreign legation, or someone else with whom he could discuss state business of the moment.

The effect of Dolly's week-to-week appearance on American styles cannot be exaggerated. When she wore a train, trains became the rage; when she revealed her cleavage, necklines dropped everywhere; when she wore blue—or green or red or yellow—that color became the color favored by thousands. Her tastes were less extreme than those of Pauline Bonaparte, Napoleon's sister, and far more vivacious than those of his second wife, the stodgy Empress Marie Louise, so Washington City became an important fashion center—a position it lost when Madison's second term ended, and he retired permanently to the country with his wife.

The Wednesday drawing rooms were more than frivolous social events that one attended in order to see and be seen. Men of substance and standing soon learned they could do business with their peers more effectively over a dish of ice cream than in an office. And there was always the chance that one could enjoy a private word with the President, who was so busy that Edward Coles sometimes scheduled his appointments as far as three weeks in advance.

Mrs. John Tyler, a First Lady who lived in the White House a quarter of a century later, said that "Dolly Madison added a new dimension to Washington society." Certainly the frontier town on the Potomac stabilized, matured, and developed a previously unknown polish during the years of the Madison Administration. People gained a respect for the Presidency as an institution that had been lacking during the early years of the Republic, when the Founding Fathers had stressed the democratic foundations on which American society rested.

The United States was still absorbing the vast Louisiana Territory and had not yet embarked on the expansionist thrust that, by midcentury, would place her continental limits on the Pacific Ocean. And not until immigrants by the millions came to her shores in the decades immediately following the Civil War would she live up to her industrial potential and become a great world power.

But she had already earned a place of honor among the nations of the world. James Madison, as his authoritative biographer, Irving Brant, has emphasized, had already proved to the European powers that he was an exceptionally able, tough negotiator, and the American people took pride in his achievements on their behalf. Now, thanks to Dolly Madison, Washington City—the nation's show window—had come of age socially, too.

XVIII

*A*s the nineteenth century's first decade drew to its close, the United States was a growing nation, increasingly aware of its rich natural resources. Only the increasing threat of war with Great Britain dimmed her promise and created a serious internal problem—the secession movement in New England. In spite of these difficulties President Madison knew, as did former President Jefferson and others who had been responsible for the establishment of the Republic, that the American experiment in democratic government was a success.

Census-taking methods were crude, but it was estimated that the nation now had a total population of approximately 7.5 million. The Boston Athenaeum was flourishing as a center of scholarship and culture, the Theatre d'Orleans had been built in New Orleans as the home of grand opera at a staggering cost of $100,000, and Noah Webster had published the first American-edited English-language dictionary.

Robert Fulton's steamboats were making regular runs between New York and Albany on the Hudson River, and plans were being made for the construction of the Erie Canal, which would open the West to commercial traffic. John Jacob Astor formed his first fur-trading company, and Thomas Jefferson, relieved of his political burdens, devoted himself to scientific agricultural pursuits, particularly the introduction of techniques that would prevent soil erosion.

Meanwhile the Madisons faced a personal problem. Before they left Washington City to spend the summer of 1809 at Montpelier, they realized their house was no longer large enough to accommodate the increased number of guests whom the President would be required to entertain during his sojourn in the country. Architect William Thornton, the designer of the Capitol, was an old friend and F Street neighbor. As a favor, he designed two new wings for the house.

Latrobe volunteered to supervise the project, and Jefferson offered to his old friends the services of the Monticello brickmakers. Work was started in mid-July, immediately after the Madisons arrived home, and they were again surrounded by artisans.

In addition to the new wings, extensive repairs were made on the foundations of the original house, and the chimneys were rebuilt. Dolly's pride was a colonnade built over the old icehouse. The icehouse was used to preserve ice cream for long periods and keep drinks cool. The President was so intrigued by the ingenious device that he took personal charge of the project and spent several days in the open, supervising the work of the carpenters.

Margaret Bayard Smith gave posterity its most complete picture of summer life at Montpelier during the years of Madison's Presidency. She and her husband were entertained there in August, 1809, at a time, according to Dolly, when "only" twenty-three relatives and guests were living under the Madison roof. Mrs. Smith wrote:

It was near five o'clock when we arrived, we were met at the door by Mr. Madison who led us in to the dining

(197)

room where some gentlemen were still smoking segars and drinking wine. Mrs. Madison enter'd the moment afterwards, and after embracing me, took my hand, saying with a smile, I will take you out of this smoke to a pleasanter room. She took me thro' the tea room to her chamber, which opens from it.

Everything bespoke comfort, I was going to take my seat on the sopha, but she said I must lay down on her bed, and rest myself, she loosened my riding habit, took off my bonnet, and we threw ourselves on her bed. Wine, ice, punch and delightful pineapples were immediately brought. No restraint, no ceremony. Hospitality is the presiding genius of this house, and Mrs. Madison is kindness personified. . . .

The house seemed immense. It is a large two-story house of 80 or 90 feet in length, and above 40 deep. Mrs. Cutts soon came in with her sweet children, and afterwards Mr. Madison, Mr. Cutts, and Mr. Smith. The door opening into the tea room being open, they without ceremony joined their wives. They only peeked in on us; we then shut the door and after adjusting our dress, went out on the Piazza—it is 60 feet long. Here we walked and talked until called to tea, or rather supper, for tho' tea hour, it was supper fare. The long dining table was spread, and besides tea and coffee, we had a variety of warm cakes, bread, cold meats and pastry. At table I was introduced to Mr. William Madison, brother to the President, and his wife, and three or four other ladies and gentlemen all near relatives, all plain country people, but frank, kind, warm-hearted Virginians. At this house I realized being in Virginia, Mr. Madison plain, friendly, communicative, and unceremonious as any Virginia Planter could be—Mrs. Madison, uniting to all the elegance and polish of fashion, the unadulterated simplicity, frankness, warmth, and friendliness of her native character and native state.

*Their mode of living, too, if it had more elegance than
is found among the planters, was characterized by that
abundance, that hospitality, and that freedom we are
taught to look for on a Virginia plantation. We did not sit
long at this meal—the evening was warm and we were
glad to leave the table. The gentlemen went to the
piazza, the ladies, who all had children, to their chambers, and I sat with Mrs. Madison till bed time, talking
of Washington. When the servant appeared with candles
to show me my room, she insisted on going up stairs with
me, assisted me to undress and chatted till I got into
bed. How unassuming, how kind is this woman. How
can any human being be her enemy. Truly, in her there
is to be found no gall, but the pure milk of human kindness. If I may say so, the maid was like the mistress; she
was very attractive all the time I was there, seeming as
if she could not do enough, and was very talkative. As
her mistress left the room, 'You have a good mistress,
Nany,' said I. 'Yes,' answered the affectionate creature
with warmth, 'the best I believe in the world—I would
not change her for any mistress in the whole country.'*

*The next morning Nany called me to a late breakfast,
brought me ice and water (this is universal here, even in
taverns), and assisted me to dress. We sat down between
15 and 20 persons to breakfast—and to a most excellent
Virginia breakfast—tea, coffee, hot wheat bread, light
cakes, a pone, or corn loaf—cold ham, nice hashes, chick-
ens, etc.*

In mid-August President Madison received word that
the worsening relations with Great Britain required his
immediate presence in Washington City. He spent three
days on the road, remained at the White House for a
scant seventy-two hours, and then needed another three
days for the journey back to Virginia. While he was in
the capital, he summoned the Cabinet to a meeting, stud-

ied diplomatic dispatches at length, and, as he wrote Dolly, had no time whatever for social visits. "Everything round and within reminds me that you are absent," he wrote to her, "and makes me anxious to quit this solitude."

A short time after his return to Montpelier, Secretary and Mrs. Gallatin arrived for a visit, and a few days later went with the Madisons to Monticello, where Jefferson and twelve members of his family awaited them. The President, the former President, and the Secretary of the Treasury who served both conferred for hours at a time in the library, but left no record of their talks. They did, however, find ample time to walk in the nearby woods and play with Jefferson's grandchildren. The First Lady was as relaxed as she was at Montpelier, and ran foot races with the older girls.

By the time the Madisons returned to Washington City in October, the social style that would set the precedent for all future administrations was entrenched. Jefferson had been casual to the point of sloppiness in a deliberate and successful attempt to counter the semi-royal pomposity of John Adams. Now, however, something more was needed, something that would make the Presidency a symbol of stature to Americans and foreigners alike without going to extremes.

Dolly Madison, acting with her husband's admiring approval, brewed the right mixture, and her touch was so light that most people failed to realize she was creating a new image. At social gatherings the President stood apart from other Americans. At the same time he was courteous and affable and eschewed formality. He was an "ordinary citizen" who was temporarily holding a high office.

Only American dishes were served at White House dinners, balls, and receptions. Chef Sioussa was capable of preparing gourmet European menus that would have won approval at the royal tables of Great Britain and

France. Instead he supervised the cooking of New England clam chowder and brown bread, Pennsylvania pepperpot, she-crab soup from South Carolina, the fried chicken of Maryland, and the smoked ham of Virginia. Everyone who ate at the White House during the years of the Madison Administration knew he was dining on native American fare.

Gradually, almost imperceptibly, Dolly expanded her guest list to include persons other than politicians and foreign diplomats. Washington Irving, the only American author who was regarded as a literary figure in Europe, was a guest. So were inventor Robert Fulton, portrait painter Charles Willson Peale, and actor George F. Cooke, among many others. Dolly followed the principle of extending White House invitations to men of talent in many fields, as well as to ladies of beauty, charm, and wit. America and the world approved, and other First Ladies followed in her footsteps, but not until the time of Theodore Roosevelt at the turn of the twentieth century did such brilliant companies again assemble at the White House.

It is impossible to determine whether Dolly set her patterns with deliberate forethought or followed the dictates of her own generous instincts. Although her education had been limited, she had developed a lively interest in many fields of human endeavor, and she had a genius for drawing out her guests. She had spent eight years learning the art of being a successful hostess when her husband had been Secretary of State, and now, as First Lady, she applied the lessons she had taught herself.

For the first time the people of the United States wanted to know the identities of White House visitors, and each week Edward Coles provided the press with a list of prominent guests at dinners and Wednesday drawing rooms. But those who had private, urgent business with the President were left unmentioned. Dolly reserved the right to conceal any data that might embarrass her husband or create jealousies within the government.

The reemergence of James Monroe as a major political figure created special problems for the Madisons. Secretary of State Smith was so inept that many members of the Congress openly urged the President to discharge him, and Monroe was the logical man to take his place. But Madison and the former envoy continued to hold each other at arm's length, even though they had ostensibly buried the hatchet immediately prior to the election of 1808. Jefferson and Gallatin were among the many who suggested that Madison get rid of Smith and give Monroe the State Department.

In January, 1811, Monroe took office as governor of Virginia, a signal that he had returned to public life. He and the President opened a tentative correspondence, but both men remained on their guard. That summer Dolly broke the ice by conquering her dislike of Elizabeth Monroe sufficiently to go with her husband to Albemarle, the Monroe home. Soon thereafter relations between the men mended rapidly, and Monroe resigned the governorship in order to accept appointment as Secretary of State, a post he filled with distinction as long as Madison remained in the White House.

The renewed affiliation of their husbands made it necessary for Dolly and Elizabeth to see each other frequently. Both were the seasoned wives of politicians, and they were so successful in establishing a facade of cordiality that many of their Washington City and Virginia contemporaries took it for granted that they were close friends. Only their respective intimates knew better.

A new element came to the fore in American politics on the eve of the War of 1812. Most of the Founding Fathers had either died or retired, and their places were being taken in the Congress by vigorous newcomers, many from the West, who called themselves the Young Republicans. John Randolph referred to them scathingly as "the boys" and, because of their eagerness to do battle with Great Britain, "the War Hawks."

Prominent in the group were Henry Clay of Kentucky, whose colleagues elected him Speaker of the House, and Felix Grundy of Tennessee, who became chairman of the important House Committee on Foreign Relations. They gave the President their support, because he refused to accept British demands that would have humiliated the United States.

The energetic War Hawks, who had no patience with protocol and were indifferent to tradition, had little in common with the dignified Madison, Father of the Constitution. But they were important to his cause, so Dolly did her part to bind them to him. In 1811 each War Hawk received several invitations to White House dinners and Wednesday drawing rooms. Dolly dazzled them. The rarely impetuous Clay called her "the most charming of ladies it has ever been my good fortune to encounter." Thanks in part to his wife's efforts, Madison received the unqualified support of the Young Republicans in his successful 1812 bid for reelection and in legislation designed to strengthen his hand after the war broke out.

As the President's tension increased and his work day lengthened, his wife became even more important to him. Dolly continued to observe her usual morning routine of dressing inconspicuously and wearing no cosmetics as she went to the local markets to do her own shopping for food and other supplies. Then she hurried back to the White House in time to change into something more attractive before the President joined her at noon.

No longer eating their main dinner at midday, largely because Madison became too sleepy, the couple had a "light, late breakfast" served to them in their private sitting room. Only on rare occasions did anyone join them or did they go to the dining room with a larger group. The President desperately needed an hour of relaxation and was soothed by his wife's company. Edward Coles observed that he often looked harassed before joining Dolly for lunch, but that he had become "serene" by the time he returned to his office. She allowed nothing to interfere with her immediate availability when her husband needed her help.

Madison was feeling the weight of his office and slept so poorly that he and Dolly now occupied separate, adjoining chambers. He read late, awoke frequently, and sometimes spent the better part of the night reading or wandering around his bedroom. Dolly kept a large candle burning all night on his dressing table so he wouldn't stumble in the dark. And, symbolically, she invariably left the door open between their rooms.

Dinner was served in the evening, and Dolly conserved the President's strength by giving parties no more often than two nights each week, when she made certain that ladies of intelligence and humor were seated near him. On the other nights, when only family members were present, she conversed with him herself throughout the meal, usually rising once or twice to refill his wineglass.

Madison was almost sixty years old as the war approached, and he looked his age. Dolly, at forty-three, was still as beautiful as she was lively, although she would have been regarded as overweight by the standards of a later age. The couple continued to surround themselves with young people. Robert and Alfred Madison, the President's nephews, lived at the White House for months at a time, as did John Payne, Dolly's young brother, and her son, Payne Todd, now a young man and badly spoiled. Lucy Washington was there, too, and Washington Irving called her "the most popular widow in a city filled with widows of the great and the rich."

Often the children of friends, young people in their late teens and early twenties, were invited to the White House for visits, and Irving observed that the "stately mansion was filled with youthful laughter." With war now inevitable and the United States woefully unprepared, Madison was desperately in need of good cheer.

XIX

*P*resident Madison made every effort to rally and unite his people on the eve of war, and when it was learned that Great Britain was engaged in secret attempts to persuade New England to secede, he shared the wild indignation of the War Hawks. The able John C. Calhoun, a Republican-Democrat from South Carolina, made an open offer on the floor of the House of Representatives to fight a duel with any member who favored secession. That night the President drank a toast to Calhoun with wine provided by Henry Clay.

But opportunities for enjoyment were few, and the President was so busy that Dolly let it be known they would accept no invitations to any functions, public or private, held outside the White House. Madison's appearances at the Wednesday drawing rooms became shorter, and after his wife's dinners, he usually disappeared into his study, accompanied by any Cabinet members, Young Republicans, or senior Senators who happened to be present.

The one gala event of the season was the wedding, on March 29, 1812, of Lucy Payne Washington to Supreme Court Justice Thomas Todd. Between them the bride and groom had eight children, all of whom were members of the wedding party, as were the many young people living in the White House. Dolly managed the wedding with her usual brilliance, holding it in the large East Room because so many guests had been invited. The bride coaxed the President to dance with her, and the entire company—Dolly included—applauded him. It was the first time anyone had seen him dance since he had become President.

Vice President George Clinton died on April 20, and the Madisons attended his funeral. Dolly was outraged because several gentlemen of prominence attempted to engage in "politicking" with the President before Clinton was lowered into his grave.

The President was encountering difficulties in finding lieutenants, other than Gallatin and Monroe, on whom he could rely. Congressman Cutts was ill in Maine, and Dolly's other brother-in-law, John G. Jackson, had resigned his seat in the House. William Pinkney, the new Attorney General, was an energetic, able man, but spent most of his time in Baltimore. Secretaries Eustis and Hamilton of the War and Navy Departments were proving themselves incapable of making adequate preparations for war, and the President, not wanting to create a stir by discharging them, asked the Congress for the right to appoint assistant secretaries, but his request was refused.

Dolly showed the strain in her own way, complaining in a letter to Anna that Washingtonians in high places were taking unfair advantage of White House hospitality. They gave no parties of their own, but unfailingly showed up for her dinners, thus taxing the strength of "my dear husband [who] is overpowered with business."

Life was further complicated by the approach of the 1812 Presidential election. Madison, in firm control of his party's rank-and-file and unstintingly supported by the Young Republicans, seemed certain of reelection. But Federalist hopes revived when they nominated the energetic Mayor De Witt Clinton of New York, nephew of the late

Vice President, and named Jared Ingersoll, a virtual un-known, as his running mate.

The Republican-Democratic Congressional caucus, held under Clay's energetic leadership, resulted in the nom-ination of Governor Elbridge Gerry of Massachusetts as the candidate for Vice President, and Madison was de-lighted. Gerry was a distinguished patriot, a fellow Found-ing Father, and would enlist considerable support in Fed-eralist New England. In addition he was too old to pose a serious threat to the Presidential hopes of James Mon-roe in 1816.

Too busy to participate actively in a campaign, the President was content to leave politics to Gerry and the editors of Republican-Democratic newspapers. He be-lieved—and Jefferson, Monroe, and Gallatin agreed—that he would be reelected even if the Federalists captured all of the New England states, New York, and some of the smaller eastern states. His own constituency was solid in the South and West, where the demands for war were becoming shrill.

The President faced the grave possibility of fighting simultaneous wars against Great Britain and France, both of the major European combatants being unscrupulous in violating the rights of American merchantmen. He con-sulted at length with Secretary Monroe, former President Jefferson, and Speaker Clay, and spent such long hours at his desk that Dolly was afraid his health would give way. Ultimately he reached a sensible decision with which his friends agreed: The United States was too weak to fight Britain and France at the same time, and therefore would be wise to direct her entire effort against the more virulently aggressive of her foes, Britain.

On June 1, 1812, President Madison sent a special message to the Senate and House of Representatives re-questing a declaration of war. On June 18 the Congress declared war against Great Britain, and Dolly wept when a courier brought word of it to the White House.

Commander-in-Chief Madison had approved of war only as a last resort, and now he used all of his strength to prepare for the ordeal ahead. But he was thwarted by the New England Federalists, who stubbornly refused to cooperate with the national government. The Navy, although badly outnumbered, fought brilliantly and gave a nation hungry for victory its chief satisfaction. The Army, poorly led, ill trained, and inadequately supplied, stumbled at first from one disaster to the next. Generals Henry Dearborn in the East and William Hull in the West were too old for their commands, and America was soon shaken by the news of severe defeats and heavy losses in dead, wounded, and prisoners captured.

The heat of Washington City became unbearable, but neither the President nor his wife thought of going to Montpelier for their annual sojourn. Madison worked eighteen to twenty hours each day, and Dolly canceled all social engagements. The only meals served to outsiders at the White House were working dinners with subordinates who were spending endless evenings with the President.

Working unceasingly in a vain effort to find competent field commanders, Madison exhausted himself. Dolly finally intervened, and he consented to accompany her to Montpelier for a scant two weeks early in September. While there, however, he maintained the same punishing schedule, taking no respite.

He had no time to take part in the election campaign, delivering no addresses and making no public appearances. Members of the Congress and of Republican-Democratic state organizations did all the work, and Madison was devoting so much of his time and effort to war-related matters that he held only a few political conferences.

Certainly the outcome was never in doubt, which may be one reason he paid so little attention to the election. New England lined up solidly against him, in spite of Gerry's appearance on the ticket as his running mate. But the South gave him solid support, as did the West, an indication to the experienced that the new states across the mountains held the balance of power.

The President received 128 Electoral College votes to 89 for De Witt Clinton. Gerry won the Vice Presidency by an almost identical vote, receiving 131 to 86 for Ingersoll. There was no celebration at the White House on December 2, when the final results became known, and the President conducted business as usual.

The country having given him a mandate to conduct the war as he saw fit, Madison found Cabinet replacements for the all-important war ministries. The Navy Department was given to William Jones, a wealthy Philadelphia merchant and Republican-Democratic stalwart, who had been a sea captain and consequently had a thorough understanding of the need for ships, trained men, and armaments that would enable the United States to meet the Royal Navy on more equal terms. The War Department portfolio went to John Armstrong of New York, who had just returned home after serving as minister to France. He had been a brigadier general at one time and supposedly knew the Army's needs, but neither he nor anyone else could produce new military leadership overnight.

Dolly gave a small dinner party for the Cabinet members and their wives and found the new additions pleasant. There was obvious friction between Monroe and Armstrong, however, and their relations were further hampered by friction between their ladies. Mrs. Armstrong was sophisticated, and Dolly, who enjoyed her company, may have secretly sided with her. But she was careful to play no favorites. Her husband leaned heavily on James

Monroe for help, and she knew better than to allow a women's feud to cause problems on the top level of the administration.

The Cutts family returned to Washington with a new baby, their fourth living child, and moved back into the White House for what proved to be their last winter there. Richard Cutts had been defeated for reelection, and in January, 1813, his brother-in-law appointed him to an important new War Department post, superintendent of military supplies. In the spring Anna Cutts found a Washington City house suitable for her family, and they vacated the White House wing they had been occupying. Dolly continued to see her sister almost daily, however, and they remained very close.

Payne Todd, who was now 22 years old, was a growing cause of concern. He had just been graduated from the school in Baltimore, but showed no interest in following in his stepfather's footsteps and attending Princeton. For a few months in 1813 he acted as a member of the White House staff, particularly during the illness of Edward Coles, but he was far more interested in spending money on clothes and girls, and the Madisons became increasingly worried. Finally, in April, 1813, the President found a solution.

Imperial Russia having offered to act as a mediator in the war between America and Great Britain, Madison sent Secretary Gallatin to Europe as a special commissioner authorized to investigate the possibilities of such an arrangement. Payne Todd was made an official member of the Gallatin party and received the title of secretary to the commissioner. But the young man showed no improvement. Freed from the disciplines that had restricted him at boarding school, he spent money in Europe more rapidly than his mother and stepfather could refill his purse. He frequently contracted substantial debts, apparently realizing that his family would be obliged to pay them because a failure to assume responsibility for him would have embarrassed the President of the United States.

Two young newcomers to the White House helped the President forget his cares. One was Dolly's cousin, Betsy Coles, the sister of Edward, who treated Madison with irreverence and loved to tease him. She remained close to both Dolly and her husband for the rest of their lives. The other guest was a fellow Virginian, Maria Mayo, who was equally attractive and whose popularity with young officers rivaled Betsy's. At the end of the war she married a young officer who had served with distinction, Brigadier General Winfield Scott, who was destined to become commanding general of the U.S. Army, field commander in the Mexican War, and ultimately unsuccessful candidate for the Presidency.

The war curtailed the social activities of Washington City, so the ladies, led by Dolly, took up a new pastime. The two greatest orators of the day were Speaker Henry Clay and Attorney General William Pinkney, and Dolly made it fashionable to sit in the gallery of the House of Representatives when Clay was scheduled to make an address, or to attend a session of the Supreme Court when Pinkney argued a case there.

The war was not allowed to interfere with the festivities held in honor of the President's second inaugural. The customary ball was held on the night of March 4, 1813, but the President had to return to his desk, so he and Dolly departed immediately after supper. The next night an "imperial" ball was given for them at the Russian legation. Again duty compelled the President to leave early, but on this occasion Dolly did not accompany him. She remained until the party ended in the small hours of the morning. For this the Federalist newspapers criticized her, hinting broadly that she had been guilty of conduct unworthy of a First Lady. The charges were groundless, and the Madisons paid no attention to the press barrage.

Only one member of the family took notice of the attack. Dolly's brother-in-law, John G. Jackson, had returned to the House of Representatives that winter and delivered a scathing counterassault in an angry speech, charging that the Federalists were trying to impair the prestige of the President by unfairly smearing his wife. The Federalists had gone too far, as most members of the Congress realized, and the matter was dropped.

The President continued to work seven days and nights each week, and in June, 1813, his health gave way. He suffered from a raging fever, for which his physicians prescribed quinine. Dolly allowed no one else to nurse him and for three weeks never left his side. The physicians were optimistic that he would recover, but she did not share their opinion, and for days at a time she was in despair.

She allowed Madison to see no visitors, including Cabinet members, and as a consequence wild rumors filled Washington City. It was commonly assumed that the President was dying, and not even Secretary of State Monroe could assure his colleagues and members of the Congress that the stories were false.

By early July Madison passed the crisis, and Dolly wrote that the worst was behind him, confessing, "Now that I see him get well I feel as if I might die myself from fatigue." She displayed remarkable recuperative powers, however, and within a few days showed no ill effects of the ordeal.

But the convalescence of the sixty-two-year-old President was slow. On July 3 Dolly allowed Secretary Monroe to see him for a short time, and thereafter she admitted other Cabinet members to his bedchamber, too, but she kept a close watch and would not permit him to work too hard. Not until mid-July did she permit Congressional leaders to visit him.

The physicians urged Madison to leave Washington City as soon as possible, and Dolly made plans for a protracted journey to Montpelier. Her husband said he was too busy to go, but she tolerated no nonsense from him, paid no attention to his protests, and in August literally had him carried to his coach for the trip.

By the end of August the President's health was restored, and Dolly wrote that he was "perfectly well, but will be better for another month on the mountain." Cabinet members were urging Madison to return to Washington City, but Dolly would not hear of his premature departure, insisting that he remain until the beginning of October.

The war was always close at hand. The President received daily dispatches and sent large numbers of messages in return as he increasingly took charge of the government's affairs. But Dolly continued to hover over him and managed to reestablish many of the prewar routines. She encouraged her husband to take his customary morning ride around his estate, and visits were exchanged with the Jefferson family. There were numerous members of the Madison and Payne clans staying at Montpelier, plus a heavy influx of official visitors, but Dolly coped with everyone and every situation, shielding the President at every turn.

By the time they returned to Washington City early in October, the President's health was excellent. The war news remained gloomy, however, and Dolly was furious because New England newspapers now referred to the conflict as "Mr. Madison's war." His enemies, she wrote to Hannah Gallatin, were "vicious and unfair." Many New Englanders and most Europeans regarded the New World conflict as a minor adjunct to the titanic struggle between Napoleon and Britain, which was reaching its climax. But James Madison—and with him his wife—knew that a defeated America might be dismembered by European powers, who would reassert their domination of former colonies. The War of 1812, the President knew, was the final phase of the War of Independence.

Meanwhile, military victories were few, and, early in 1814, Madison accepted a private British offer to conduct direct peace negotiations. The American team appointed by the President consisted of Gallatin, John Quincy Adams, and James Bayard, who were already in Europe, along with Henry Clay and Jonathan Russell. His decision to negotiate was wise. However, even before the appointment of the commission was announced, the British decisively defeated Napoleon. They were now in a position to send the bulk of their mammoth fleet as well as thousands of veteran divisions to deal with the New World upstarts. There was no armistice, the fighting continued, and the American people were alarmed.

XX

*I*t is unlikely that Dolly Madison, at the age of forty-six, imagined herself as the perpetrator of heroic deeds. Her place in history as a First Lady already secure, she was the war-weary wife of a beleaguered President. She did what was required of a woman in the limelight, but her husband's health was still her first concern, and she tried to ease his burden by entertaining infrequently and simply, acting as a buffer between him and people who would have wasted his time and energies. It was a combination of circumstances and her own character that made her a heroine.

By the time the Congress adjourned in the spring of 1814, the President had appointed a number of new, vigorous Army leaders, including Major General Andrew Jackson of Tennessee, an Indian fighter who was given the command in the West, with headquarters in New Orleans. The Madisons paid their first spring visit to Montpelier since they had been living in the White House, and by the time they returned to Washington City in June, the President's worst fears were being realized. Definite information had been received to the effect that the British were sending a corps of veteran troops and a powerful fleet to force an American surrender.

In July, 1814, the vanguard of a Royal Navy fleet and a large number of British troop transports appeared in Chesapeake Bay, carrying land forces under the command of General Robert Ross, an exceptionally able officer. Secretary of War Armstrong insisted that Baltimore —home port for many privateersmen and a far more strategic target than the dusty little village-capital—was the enemy's real object. But the President and Secretary of State Monroe felt certain the British intended to attack Washington.

The inhabitants of the town shared that belief. As Dolly wrote to Hannah Gallatin, the city was

'in a state of perturbation . . . the depradations of the Enemy approaching within miles . . . and the disaffected making incessant difficulties for the government. Such a place as this has become I cannot describe it. I wish we were at Philadelphia. The people here do not deserve that I should prefer it—among other exclamations and threats they say that if Mr. Madison attempts to move from this House in case of an attack they will stop him, and that he shall fall with it. I am not the least alarmed at these things, but entirely disgusted, and determined to stay with him.'

The British continued to build up their strength, and a special capital defense district was created and placed under the command of General William H. Winder. Secretary Armstrong believed in him, but events would prove Winder to be totally inefficient. In all justice to him, however, posterity has concluded that he had no time to transform his corps of raw, untrained recruits into a real fighting force.

On the morning of August 17 Dolly sent a brief letter to Hannah Gallatin, saying she had sent the Gallatin silver and other valuables to Philadelphia for safekeeping. She acted just in time.

That same day a fleet of fifty-six British warships, including twenty-one transports carrying 4,000 veteran troops, anchored at the mouth of the Patuxent River, a scant thirty-five miles from Washington City. A ferocious artillery barrage cleared the area of General Winder's recruits, and General Ross established a beachhead.

When the news reached Washington City before dawn the next day, Secretary Armstrong continued to insist it was Baltimore the enemy intended to attack. President Madison and Secretary Monroe knew better. The previous year an American column had burned down the Houses of Parliament in York, Canada—later to be known as Toronto—and it was obvious to them that General Ross planned to return the compliment.

By August 22 the enemy's precise intentions were as yet unclear, but Madison was becoming increasingly apprehensive. He ordered the government's archives carried off into Virginia, and after deciding to visit General Winder's corps himself, he asked Dolly if she was afraid to stay in the White House without him. She replied that she had no fear either for herself or for him, and she promised him she would see to it that Cabinet papers "both public and private" would be preserved intact.

By the time the President returned on the evening of August 23, the situation had become worse. The British landing had been virtually unopposed and was complete.

By this time Dolly had herself loaded all of the Cabinet papers into a carriage, and the President ordered the documents taken off to Virginia. Many Washingtonians considered Madison personally responsible for the enemy landing, and by this time a large hostile crowd had gathered outside the White House.

Secretary Monroe was so disgusted with the inefficiency of Winder's regiments that he was acting as the chief American field scout, and soon after midnight on the morning of August 24 the President received a scribbled message from him: The British were marching on Washington, and all bridges should be burned.

Madison ordered General Winder to rally his forces and hold the British, no matter what the cost. At the same time he prepared to evacuate his capital, rightly placing no faith in Winder's corps. There is no clear record of what transpired during the rest of the frantic night, but at one point Madison tried to persuade Dolly to leave at once for Virginia.

She refused, saying she would not budge until she knew he would be safe.

Before dawn the President received a message from the frenzied Winder, whose men were retreating. The President, armed with a pair of dueling pistols, rode off to join the members of his Cabinet at the American field headquarters, where Monroe was trying to move two regiments of Maryland militia into the line. Only the intervention of a young sergeant on sentry duty prevented the President from riding by accident into the enemy camp, where he would have suffered the ultimate humiliation of capture.

The main battle, if it can be dignified by that name, was fought around noon. Many of Winder's recruits fled without firing a single shot, the American lines buckled, and the British advanced so rapidly they were forced to halt and regroup their forces. During this respite President Madison, accompanied by a small escort, raced back toward his threatened capital.

It was at this time that Dolly Madison became a heroine.

Anxiously awaiting word from her husband, she sat down at 1:30 P.M. to a light meal of cold meats, bread, and cheese. Before she had taken more than a bite or two, however, the thunder of cannon fire in the distance told her all she needed to know.

Racing into the open, she commandeered a large wagon, ordered her own small carriage brought to the door, and then half-bullied, half-shamed several surly Washingtonians into helping her. She loaded the last of the Presidential papers into the wagon, then filled it with the White House silver and china, and the draperies of red velvet that had been her pride in the main drawing room. In great haste she also carried several armloads of books to the wagon.

Meanwhile, the sound of artillery fire grew louder.

A close friend, Matilda Love, whose husband was in the field commanding a battalion of Maryland infantry, arrived to tell Dolly she could tarry no longer. Paying no attention to the advice, Dolly would not go while there was still space in the wagon and her carriage for valuables.

Aided by Matilda, she carried eight or nine official White House paintings to the wagon, among them portraits of Presidents Adams and Jefferson. A young lieutenant galloped up to the door and begged her to hurry.

Dolly borrowed his knife, cut the famous portrait of President Washington by Gilbert Stuart from its frame, and took it with her into her carriage. The only personal item she took was a small French clock her husband had given her as a wedding present. As she herself later wrote, she was forced to leave behind "everything else belonging to the public," as well as her own clothes and jewelry, her husband's belongings, food and wines she had purchased, and everything owned by the servants. In this hour of peril it did not occur to her to salvage her own things. Her sole concern was that of saving White House property that had already become a part of America's heritage.

At last she and Matilda drove off together, with Dolly holding the reins. They were closely followed by the lieutenant, who drove the wagon.

No more than a half hour later, around three P.M., President Madison arrived, accompanied only by an aide, and found the White House deserted. The table was still set, and he ate a chunk of bread while scribbling instructions to Secretary Jones to destroy the stores in the Navy Yard.

Assuming that Dolly and other members of the family would meet him in Georgetown, the President hurried there but could not find them. So, after leaving instructions that they were to join him in Virginia, he went to Alexandria by ferry. Those who saw him later described his poise as remarkable.

According to tradition, General Ross and some of his subordinate commanders found the food on the table, ate it, and then drank a toast to Madison, their "future prisoner," before British troops set fire to the White House. After dark, fires were also lighted at the Treasury, the State Department, and the War Department. The flames were plainly visible from vantage points in the Virginia hills.

A number of legends about Dolly Madison's conduct the rest of that day and night have added to her fame, but most appear apocryphal. It was said that when she saw Washington burning in the distance, she wept, vowing to return, but no substance can be found for the story.

According to another tale, she and Mrs. Love spent the night in the open, surrounded by a company of Maryland infantrymen who swore they would die to the last man before they allowed the Redcoats to capture the First Lady.

The actual facts, although dramatic, are less colorful. About an hour after dark Dolly and her companion found refuge at the comfortable home of a Virginia gentleman farmer with whose family the First Lady was acquainted. She was so fearful for the President's safety that the young lieutenant went in search of him.

Instead the officer encountered a half-troop of Virginia

cavalry, who accompanied him back to the farmhouse and there mounted guard over Dolly and the White House valuables. She and Mrs. Love were shown every courtesy, and as they had escaped with only the clothes they were wearing, their hostess lent them clean undergarments the following morning.

A violent thunderstorm raged in Washington City the night the British occupied the town. The rain extinguished the fires and prevented their spread to scores of other wooden buildings. General Ross was content, however. He hoped the havoc he had created would convince the American people that their nation had been defeated.

The President, after a very brief rest, was back in the saddle, trying to learn the location of Winder's army and attempting to rally his disorganized forces. He and Dolly were briefly united early that evening at a tavern near Falls Church, Virginia, where they discovered they had spent the previous night only a mile apart.

Madison went on almost immediately, crossing into Maryland, where he finally located Winder and Monroe. On the morning of August 27 he wrote a note to his wife, telling her the British had evacuated Washington City and that he was returning without delay. "You will . . . of course take the same resolution," he added.

Late that afternoon he reached his devastated capital. Only the charred walls of the White House still stood, and most public buildings had been destroyed. Dead horses littered the lawns of the Capitol, and many nearby private dwellings had been gutted, including the home of the Gallatins.

The President went on to his own house on F Street, where he found the Richard Cutts family awaiting him. He called an immediate Cabinet meeting and gave the command of the Washington military district to Monroe, the most competent of his lieutenants. Secretary Jones told him that Dolly was staying at the tavern near Falls

Church, awaiting word from him, so he wrote her another letter.

It was possible, he told her, that bargeloads of British marines might return to the city to set more fires. In that event he urged her to remain in Falls Church, saying that to flee again "would have a disagreeable effect." If the rumors about the return of the British proved false, however, "you cannot return too soon."

The conduct of Madison and his wife throughout this time of crisis was admirable. Both remained calm and cheerful, never complaining. The President refused to consider surrender to the enemy, and when a lady in Falls Church asked Dolly what would become of the United States now, she was told in no uncertain terms, "We shall rebuild Washington City. The enemy cannot frighten a free people."

Late on the night of August 27 the President and Secretary Monroe returned to the house on F Street after inspecting the cannon emplaced along the banks of the Potomac River to repel another invasion. There, to the President's astonishment, he found Dolly waiting for him.

She had ignored his advice, and as soon as she had received his letter, she had left Falls Church in a borrowed carriage to join him. Her return to the capital, her contempt for the enemy provided the people of Washington City with the tonic they needed. Word of her arrival spread quickly, and in spite of the late hour large crowds turned out to cheer her. She responded by smiling, waving, and occasionally shaking her fist toward the north, where the British had marched.

A number of people offered the Madisons the use of their houses, but they declined, preferring to be in their own home, which instantly became the nerve center of the government. A platoon of cavalry was assigned to permanent guard duty, and both the President and the First Lady went to work.

Madison immediately discharged the incompetent Armstrong, giving the War Department portfolio to the overburdened Monroe, who added the direction of the war effort to his duties as Secretary of State. Meanwhile Dolly visited every burned and gutted building, and initiated a campaign in which she asked for volunteers to rebuild the capital.

Overnight she became a valuable political asset to her harassed husband, who was blamed by many for the British capture and destruction of Washington City. Her heroism in taking White House valuables to safety at the last possible moment while leaving her own belongings behind was a story told and retold in every American newspaper. She was hailed, too, for her courage in returning to the capital before the danger ended. Soon volunteers were descending on Washington City by the hundreds from every part of the Eastern Seaboard to assist in the rebuilding of the town. Thanks at least in part to Dolly, the attempt of the British to destroy the spirit of Americans badly misfired and had the opposite effect.

Seasoned politicians soon discovered that Dolly sought no glory for herself. Her patriotism was genuine, as real and deep-rooted as her concern for her husband's good name, and admiration for her cut across party lines.

On September 1 the President issued a proclamation urging all citizens to unite in an effort to "chastise and repel the invader." Determined to remain in Washington City, so the American people and the enemy alike would know the United States government could not be driven away, Madison resisted suggestions that the capital be moved elsewhere on a temporary basis. The Patent Office and the Post Office were the only government buildings that had not been damaged, and he ordered them prepared for use, later in the autumn, by the Senate and the House of Representatives.

Meanwhile an equally determined Dolly was discovering that the modest house on F Street was inadequate. Her husband needed more space for offices and conferences. The place was too cramped for the ceremonies in which the Chief Executive was required to participate, and there wasn't enough room for the social functions she was expected to give.

The French minister gallantly offered to give up the home he was renting, a spacious house on Eighteenth Street. Dolly accepted, and the Madisons moved in, accompanied by the young relatives who made up their household. The British attempt to ruin the prestige of the government had failed.

The military situation took a sharp turn for the better, too. An army of the veterans who had defeated Napoleon set out from Montreal in an attempt to invade the United States by way of the familiar New York route but was halted at Lake Champlain. The combined sea and land attack on Baltimore by the force that had sacked Washington City also was stopped and turned back.

The peace commissioners, conferring with their British counterparts at Ghent, in Belgium, were making good progress, and they reported they were inching toward an agreement in which war-weary Britain would recognize the maritime rights of the United States. But, with the end in sight, the British commissioners vacillated.

Toward the end of the year the most powerful force the British had yet sent to the New World appeared in the Gulf of Mexico, and General Andrew Jackson's regulars, militia, volunteer frontiersmen, and Indian fighters mobilized for the defense of New Orleans. In one of the ironies of history the peace treaty was signed at Ghent in the closing days of 1814, but the news wasn't received in time to prevent the Battle of New Orleans, the largest and bloodiest encounter of the war.

On January 8, 1815, Jackson won a decisive victory, demonstrating that Americans could meet the Old World's finest troops on equal terms and defeat them. The news of his triumph overshadowed the signing of the treaty, and the victory-starved people of the United States had a new hero.

Word of Jackson's achievement and the signing of the treaty reached Washington City in February, and the temporary White House became the center of a seemingly endless series of spontaneous celebrations. Madison had been completely vindicated, the New England separatists looked foolish, and it seemed to Dolly that everyone in the country wanted to shake her husband's hand and drink a toast to him.

Madison was too busy to spend much time with the celebrants and confined himself to his offices in the temporary White House. But so many visitors called each day that Dolly was forced to give the equivalent of a series of open houses. "My brain has been harried with noise and bustle," she wrote in March. "Such overflowing rooms I never saw before—I sigh for repose."

Repose was the last thing she really wanted. With her usual enthusiasm, she plunged into the task of furnishing the temporary White House, and the arrival of silks, brocades, and other materials from France soon enabled her to replace her wardrobe. By March, too, a holiday of a different sort seemed feasible. Albert and Hannah Gallatin invited her to meet them in Paris.

The prospect overwhelmed her, but her husband had other ideas. Still tired after his long years of work, he yearned for a protracted visit to his beloved Montpelier. Dolly recognized her duty, swallowed her disappointment, and accompanied him on a visit to Montpelier that began late in March and lasted for three months.

In June and early July the Madisons returned to Washington for a brief stay of a month and a half, then hurried back to Montpelier, where they learned of Napoleon's final defeat by the British at Waterloo. Peace in Europe as well as the New World was now ensured.

Not all of the news was good, however. Early in September Payne Todd returned home with the Gallatins after a stay of two years in Europe. His wardrobe was extensive and his manners were exquisite, but he was lazy, and his mother and stepfather were horrified to learn that he had accumulated more than $8,000 in debts. Presumably he had lost the money at the gaming table, and it soon became evident that card playing was his only interest.

Dolly tried to reason with her son at length, as did Madison, but their efforts were wasted. Payne was amiable, readily agreeing that he suffered shortcomings, but he made no attempt to mend his ways. The United States had won peace with honor, the President was more popular than he had ever been, and Dolly was revered as a heroine and great lady. But their joy was tempered by the knowledge that Payne's gambling was a disgrace to them and to himself.

XXI

$\mathscr{T}$he return of the Madisons to Washington City from Montpelier in early October, 1815, marked the beginning of the capital's postwar social life, and the President and First Lady enjoyed themselves thoroughly, in spite of their worry over Payne Todd. Dolly immediately resumed her Wednesday receptions, at which her husband now made only token appearances, usually showing up only a short time before each of these affairs was scheduled to end. It was common knowledge that the receptions bored him, but his absence in no way diminished their popularity. Members of the Congress, foreign diplomats, and visiting dignitaries were still flattered to receive an invitation to the White House from Dolly Madison.

A new event was added to the weekly routine. Informal dinner parties were held every Monday, with the guest list rarely numbering fewer than ten or more than twenty-five. Before the season ended early the following summer, every member of the Washington establishment had been entertained, as well as scores of prominent visitors from all parts of the United States and Europe. As always, Dolly was very much in command, making certain that the service was smooth and attentive, that there were no lags in conversation, and that no guest was ignored. Her husband was very much at ease at these dinners and chatted amiably with those seated near him. Several of the newer members of the Congress, who had not been acquainted with him in prewar years, commented that they had never seen him so relaxed. And a number discovered, for the first time, that he was endowed with a lively sense of humor.

One of the customs Dolly had inaugurated during the War of 1812 remained in effect. Under no circumstances would she and the President accept invitations to attend private parties, and the only official functions for which they left the White House were the occasional dinners for the heads of foreign legations given by Secretary and Mrs. Monroe. The Monroe cook was inferior, Dolly wrote to Anna, and the atmosphere in the home of the Secretary of State was stilted, but the mere presence of the First Lady was enlivening, and Dolly did her duty without complaint.

Madison gave Monroe his unqualified support for the Presidency but took no active part in the 1816 campaign. Dolly, like her husband, appears to have taken it for granted that Monroe would be elected. Certainly the President was surprised when William H. Crawford of Georgia received 54 votes to Monroe's 65 in a Republican-Democratic caucus of members of the Congress held in March. Thereafter, however, Monroe had clear sailing, and his Federalist opponent, Rufus King, was given no chance of winning the Presidency.

Madison thoroughly enjoyed the last year of his Presidency, and Dolly shared his pleasure. Pressures had lessened so much that they were able to go to Montpelier early in June, 1816, and they remained there until October, their longest stay in the sixteen years they had been living in Washington City. The President found it necessary to spend the better part of each day in his study and frequently worked there after supper, too, but he had the time to supervise the harvesting of his tobacco and corn crops.

Never before had so many guests been entertained at Montpelier. Relatives and friends, foreign diplomats, visitors from abroad, and administration officials came to the estate in an unending stream, but their presence created no burden on either host or hostess. Dolly followed the principle of allowing guests to spend their time as they pleased, imposing no schedule on them, so the atmosphere remained relaxed.

She gave a number of dinner parties, and more often than not the company ate outdoors. On Independence Day more than ninety persons were present for a feast spread on tables beneath the trees. Dolly observed that it was less bother to entertain a group of that size at Montpelier than it was to give a dinner for twenty-five at the White House.

In mid-October the President and First Lady returned to the capital for their last six months there. James Monroe won the election, as expected, and late in the year Dolly turned her full attention to packing the belongings that had accumulated in Washington City over the period of sixteen years. Her husband ordered a wagon train sent from Montpelier to carry their books, papers, clothes, furniture, household goods, and clothes back to Virginia.

She was so busy that she cut her social activities to a minimum in January and February, 1817, and she had no time at all for correspondence. But she continued to hold her Wednesday evening receptions, which were attended by everyone from Supreme Court justices to the lowest-ranking government clerks. An era was coming to an end, and everyone in the city wanted to pay his respects to the retiring President and his lovely wife. Washington, it was predicted, would never be the same without them.

Dolly remembered how she and her family had been inconvenienced when Thomas Jefferson had remained in the White House after his term had ended, and she was determined to turn the place over to Elizabeth Monroe on March 4, 1817. The packing was not yet finished, but she had everything carted to her own house for final sorting.

She deliberately absented herself from Monroe's inauguration, not wanting to steal the spotlight from the new First Lady, and that night the Madisons made a token appearance at the ball being given for Madison's successor.

The following night, however, Dolly and James Madison came into their own. A party was given for them in Georgetown, where the decorations consisted of "paintings and verses executed on white velvet and most richly framed." These testimonials were taken to Montpelier, where they were displayed in a special room set aside for the purpose.

Many dignitaries wanted to entertain the Madisons before they left town, and they were so inundated with invitations that they lingered in Washington City until early April. Then, with their packing finally completed, they rode off into retirement, both of them relieved that their long public life had come to an end.

Their routine at Montpelier was already well established, to be sure, and they made few changes in their way of life. The former President read, conducted a busy correspondence, and continued to exchange visits with Thomas Jefferson. He was always available to his successor, too, for purposes of consultation. He and Dolly continued to entertain frequently, and friends, relatives, and distinguished guests still came to Montpelier as they had in past years.

The Madisons were joined by Payne Todd, who solemnly promised to reform and become a Virginia planter. But he was too weak. Farm life bored him, and after a few months he departed. Thereafter he drifted, going aimlessly from one part of the United States to another, living on the reputations of his mother and stepfather, borrowing money from friends who respected them, and accumulating staggering gambling debts.

Payne became his parents' major expense, and in spite of repeated pledges to mend his ways, he continued to embarrass them. They felt honor bound to repay their friends, and several of Madison's biographers have estimated that Payne cost his stepfather more than $3,000 per year until the time of Madison's death in 1836.

Dolly sold her Philadelphia property in order to pay off some of her son's unending debts. What she failed to realize was that his gambling fever was becoming increasingly intense. He acquired debts in excess of $20,000, about which she knew nothing, and her husband shielded her from worry, secretly paying them off as best he could. Over the years Payne was imprisoned for debt on a number of occasions, and each time Madison bailed him out. Not until 1829 did Dolly begin to learn the whole truth. Even then she found it difficult to reconcile herself to the hard fact that her son was beyond redemption, that his promises were worthless, and that he lacked the power to reform.

If Payne caused his parents heartache, other members of their family gave them pleasure, and Madison's nieces and nephews were frequent visitors to Montpelier, as were the children of Anna Cutts and Lucy Washington Todd. Dolly's brother John, who was fourteen years her junior, settled on a farm in Orange County, and in Madison's latter years the younger man also acted as his brother-in-law's secretary. John Payne's daughter Annie was so fond of her aunt and uncle that she spent most of her time with them, and after Madison's death Dolly adopted the girl.

Anna's children were close to them, too, and the eldest of her sons, James Madison Cutts, visited Montpelier on his honeymoon in 1834, at which time his aunt and uncle gave a party for the newlyweds and invited more than one hundred guests. The youngest of the Cutts children, Richard, was the favorite of both Madison and Dolly, and later, after marrying a descendant of Jefferson, he enjoyed a distinguished career of his own. After Dolly became a widow, Richard Cutts acted as her financial adviser and did what he could to protect her dwindling estate from Payne Todd's raids.

The retired couple lived simply. They enjoyed good health for many years and continued to entertain frequently. Madison was now more verbose than he used to be in the presence of guests, and he usually dominated the dinner-table conversations. He discussed politics, world affairs, science, literature, and philosophy with equal ease, and Dolly invariably deferred to his opinions. Sometimes, when only members of the family were present, she still enjoyed a foot race, and on occasion she challenged her husband, who felt compelled to race her. The nieces and nephews who wrote about these contests displayed a delicate, diplomatic touch and refrained from revealing the identity of the winner.

Agriculture was the former President's predominant interest, a passion he shared with Jefferson, and over the years he more than doubled the productivity of the Montpelier acres. He became the head of a local agriculture society, and in his correspondence he stressed his conviction that America's farms would make her a great nation. He and Dolly depended on the sale of their tobacco and corn for their living, and Madison was so successful that, in spite of the financial drain imposed on them by Payne Todd, they remained comfortably secure for many years.

Montpelier was still a magnet for Americans and foreigners of consequence. John Quincy Adams paid several visits there before he was elected President, and so did Andrew Jackson and Martin Van Buren. Jackson, who liked to cultivate the image of an uncouth frontiersman, was actually a man of breeding and charm. Dolly saw through his pretense, and it was she who escorted him on a tour of Montpelier. They immediately established a friendship that endured until the end of her life. Jackson called her the greatest lady in America.

Dolly's relations with Van Buren were cordial but more restrained. The New Yorker was a widower, and because he was a shrewd opportunist, he took advantage of his situation by behaving with conspicuous gallantry toward the wives of men whose support he wanted. Dolly lacked his sophistication, but she appears to have seen through him and kept her distance. Van Buren was Jackson's political heir, but he lacked popular support of his own, and Dolly had no intention of allowing him to claim that the Madisons were his admirers. She was as zealous in her protection of her husband's reputation as she was in caring for him when he was ill.

In November, 1824, the Marquis de Lafayette, who had won the affections of all Americans because of the services he had rendered during the War of Independence, came to Virginia on a triumphal return visit to the United States. He went first to Monticello to see the ailing Jefferson, and Madison joined them. Then he came to Montpelier, where Dolly met him for the first time, and both were enchanted. Lafayette commented in a letter that "nowhere have I encountered a lady who is lovelier or more steadfast." Overwhelmed by the hospitality of the Madisons, he returned in 1825 before going back to France.

Both Dolly and her husband were crushed when Thomas Jefferson died on July 4, 1826, the fiftieth anniversary of the signing of the Declaration of Independence, which he had written. Dolly was fifty-eight years old at the time and had known him as a good friend since her earliest childhood. Her husband was even more badly upset. In 1827, a decade after he left the Presidency, he suffered from a severe case of influenza. Thereafter his health declined steadily.

Nevertheless the Madisons occasionally visited friends and relatives in the neighborhood, and in 1829, twelve years after the former President's retirement, they made a journey of consequence. Madison's Orange County neighbors elected him as a delegate to a convention that would draft a new constitution for Virginia, so he and Dolly went to Richmond, where they lived for three months with Sally Coles Stevenson, a cousin.

Madison was the only member of the group who had been a delegate to the Continental Congress in 1776, but he declined to serve as president of the convention. Instead he nominated James Monroe for the position, and his motion was seconded by Chief Justice Marshall. The three men received a standing ovation when they walked together to the podium.

The presence of so many distinguished Americans gave Richmond hostesses an opportunity they quickly seized, and parties were held almost nightly. Dolly was in her element. Although she was now sixty-one years old, her hair was still dark. Wearing her distinctive turbans, she was acclaimed the belle of the convention. One lady wrote that she looked young enough "to be Mr. Madison's daughter," and another commented that she was "as active on her feet as a girl."

However, by 1831, Madison himself was incapacitated much of the time by rheumatism, which was often accompanied by a fever. Dolly devoted herself to his welfare. She permitted no one else to nurse him, and whenever pain confined him to his bed, she refused to leave his side.

Death seemed everywhere in Madison's final years. His mother had died in 1829 at the age of ninety-seven, and no one mourned her more than her daughter-in-law, who had been her intimate friend, companion, and protector.

In 1831 the Madisons were told that the fatally ill James Monroe had quietly sold his estate and went off to spend his last months in New York with his elder daughter. In 1832 Anna Cutts died very suddenly, the unexpected tragedy sending her sister and brother-in-law to bed.

In the early winter of 1835 James Madison grew weaker and gradually lost his eyesight and hearing. Just the same, he insisted on spending his days in his favorite easy chair and was eager to converse with visitors, their numbers now restricted by a Dolly who remained constantly at his side. Late in the year she found it necessary to summon a distinguished Baltimore physician, Dr. Robley Dunglison, to attend him.

Madison rallied, but his days were numbered, and on June 28, 1836, he died at the age of eighty-five. Dolly, his wife of forty-two years, herself sixty-eight years of age, was at his bedside, as always, when he drifted into a brief sleep from which he did not awaken.

The family had been afraid Dolly would collapse, but they should have known better. She led the mourners to his graveside funeral service, walking the half-mile from the house to the cemetery, and her tears were private, concealed behind a heavy veil.

XXII

olly Madison learned gradually, over a period of months following her husband's death, that her financial situation was precarious. She was incapable of managing the plantation herself, and the money they had paid out, separately and together, to settle Payne Todd's never-ending debts, left her short of cash. Her niece, Annie Payne, whom she adopted, urged her to change her way of life, but she didn't know how to begin. Every six or eight weeks Todd sent her another request for funds, but she had nothing to give him now, and bewilderment paralyzed her.

Late in the winter of 1837 Richard Cutts came to Montpelier in the hope that he could help her straighten out her affairs. He had inherited the two-story brick house of his late parents on Lafayette Square in Washington City, and he offered her its use, free of charge, as long as she lived. He advised her to sell Montpelier, but to keep all of James Madison's correspondence and papers, saying she could obtain a good price for them. She could live on the proceeds of these sales, and he offered to manage her affairs for her, refraining from saying that he fully intended to reject the inevitable demands her son would make on her in the years ahead.

Dolly conferred at length with members of both the

Madison and Payne families, and all were agreed that Richard's idea offered the most realistic solution. She could have made her home with any one of a number of her husband's relatives or her own, but she prized her independence too much to be beholden to anyone.

Early in the spring of 1837 Richard found a buyer who offered a substantial sum for Montpelier, and Dolly was persuaded to accept it. Her personal belongings, her favorite furniture, her husband's papers, and several cartloads of mementos were collected, and in June, a year after Madison's death, Dolly left the house she had first known as a bride in 1794.

Eager nephews and nieces made the place on Lafayette Square ready for her, and she arrived in Washington City late in June, 1837, accompanied by Annie. She expected to slip into town unnoticed, but she was still Dolly Madison, and the whole town had been awaiting her coming. Less than an hour after her arrival, she was visited by her next-door neighbors, Senator and Mrs. Daniel Webster of Massachusetts, and Webster immediately assumed the role of her protector, a trust he discharged until the end of her days.

A short time later Major General and Mrs. Winfield Scott brought her a full hot dinner in heated dishes. They were followed by former President John Quincy Adams, who had returned to the Congress as a Representative from Massachusetts, and shortly after sundown President Van Buren paid a formal call on the widow of his great predecessor. That was the beginning, and in the next few weeks hundreds of calling cards were deposited on the silver tray in the front hall of the house on Lafayette Square. Twenty years had passed since Dolly had last lived in the nation's capital, but old friends had not forgotten her, and members of younger generations were eager to meet her.

In no time, or so it seemed, Dolly was engaged in an active social life. Almost seventy, she was still endowed with a limitless energy that people half her age envied. She dined frequently at the homes of John Quincy Adams and Daniel Webster and occasionally went shopping with Mrs. Adams. But she formed her closest friends with other widows.

One was Mrs. Alexander Hamilton, the daughter of Major General Philip Schuyler, who was almost eighty. She displayed an energy remarkable for her age, too, and the two ladies exchanged visits almost daily, going for carriage rides when the weather was bright.

Another friend was the widow of Mr. Stephen Decatur, the Navy hero. She had moved from the city to a small Maryland farm after her husband's death, but came into town at least once or twice each month, and at Dolly's insistence remained overnight at the house on Lafayette Square before returning to her own home.

The fourth member of the quadrumvirate was Mrs. Tobias Lear, whose late husband had been George Washington's secretary. Dolly had maintained a steady correspondence with Mrs. Lear over a period of many years, and the ladies happily renewed an old friendship.

Some Washingtonians sought Dolly's company because she was the widow of the great James Madison, but most invitations were extended for her own sake. She attended only the functions that interested her, taking care that no one took advantage of her position, but in spite of the limits she imposed on herself she was busy several evenings each week.

She could no longer afford to give her dinner parties, but one night each month she held a small reception, the size of her house making it necessary for her to hold down her guest list to thirty. She served wine, coffee, ice cream, and cookies, and overnight she reachieved the success of her

Wednesday White House socials. Dignitaries, both domestic and foreign, fought and schemed for invitations. "Mrs. Madison," President Van Buren wrote after attending one of her receptions, "is the most brilliant hostess this country has ever known."

Dolly inadvertently strengthened her ties with the Van Buren administration when one of her many grandnieces accompanied her to a White House gala. There the girl met Abraham Van Buren, the President's bachelor son and secretary; the young couple fell in love, and several months later they were married. Thereafter Dolly was invited to all family affairs at the White House.

The changes in Washington City were startling, but she accepted them with her usual aplomb. The town had more than fifty thousand inhabitants now and was still growing rapidly. The streets were not only paved but were illuminated by gas lamps, and houses were heated by coal furnaces instead of open hearths. Indoor plumbing was universal. Hotels and restaurants had proliferated, as had schools, libraries, and hospitals, and the Congress had set aside certain areas as permanent public parks.

Soon after Dolly's arrival in the capital, Richard Cutts discreetly told several prominent Senators and Representatives of her financial plight, and they stepped into the breach. The Congress voted a special bill that authorized the payment of $30,000 to Dolly for her husband's state papers covering the years from 1782 to 1787. Payne Todd's debts were so great, however, that Dolly felt compelled to pay the better part of this sum to various of his creditors.

The worst financial depression in the history of the growing nation destroyed Van Buren's second-term hopes, and General William Henry Harrison, an old Indian fighter, won the election of 1840. Dolly, who had known the Harrisons for many years, attended the inauguration on March 4, 1841, as the guest of the new President, and that night she accompanied the Harrisons to the inaugural ball. She, like the rest of the nation, was shocked when the President died a month later.

He was automatically succeeded by Vice President John Tyler of Virginia. Tyler had paid many visits to Montpelier, as had his seven sons and daughters, and the whole family leaned on Dolly for social advice. They faithfully followed her precepts of diplomatic protocol, and Mrs. Robert Tyler, who acted as her father-in-law's hostess, submitted White House guest lists for Dolly's approval until she became accustomed to Presidential routines. Daniel Webster teased Dolly at a small dinner party in his home when he observed that she was the "only permanent power in Washington." All others, he said, were transient.

In 1842 the most prominent British and American authors of the age, Charles Dickens and Washington Irving, came to Washington City, and President Tyler gave a large dinner party in their honor. The one person both wanted to meet was Dolly Madison, and they spent so much of the evening in her company that some of the other guests felt slighted.

Dolly formed the habit of attending Sunday services with Mrs. Lear at St. John's Episcopal Church. She had enjoyed no formal religious affiliation since her break with the Society of Friends at the time of her marriage in 1794. Now, however, she accepted conversion to the Episcopal Church, to which most members of the Madison and Payne families already belonged, and in 1842 her name was entered on the St. John rolls.

In April of that same year she paid her only visit to New York City, going there with Richard Cutts and Annie to sign various contracts that would permit the publication of some of James Madison's papers. New York had become the nation's largest city, and Dolly commented privately to her young relatives that she found the pace too swift. But several parties were given for her, so she enjoyed herself. She had an even better time in Philadelphia, where she paused for two weeks on her return journey to Washington. Her arrival there created a stir, and old friends gave a grand ball in her honor.

Now seventy-four years old, she was tired when she returned to the capital. The summer weather there was hot, and she gladly accepted an invitation to visit her sister, Lucy Todd, in Virginia. Following the routine she and her husband had always followed, she remained in the cool hill country until September.

On May 24, 1844, after living quietly in the capital for the better part of two more years, attending every social event of consequence, Dolly Madison again made news. Samuel F. B. Morse, the inventor of a device he called the telegraph, invited Dolly to attend a ceremony at which messages would be exchanged between Washington and Baltimore.

The first message was sent by Ann Elsworth, a young friend of the Morse family, and the inventor then invited Dolly to pass any word she wished to someone in Baltimore. She immediately thought of the wife of a Congressman who was one of her intimates, and sent the following: *Message from Mrs. Madison. She sends her love to Mrs. Wethered.* Her words subsequently appeared in newspapers throughout the world.

In 1844, James K. Polk, a Jackson disciple from Tennessee, was elected as the eleventh President of the United States. He and his wife had visited Montpelier when he was a young Congressman, and now Dolly was invited to sit with Mrs. Polk at the inauguration on March 4, 1845. The events of the day exhausted her, so she did not attend the inaugural ball that evening.

In the spring of 1845 a new crisis erupted to disturb Dolly's peaceful existence, and once again Payne Todd was responsible. He got in touch with his mother by letter, telling her he desperately needed $6,000. Annie, Richard

Cutts, and other members of the family urged her to stand firm and give him nothing.

She disagreed, largely because of her concern for her own good name and that of her late husband. She no longer entertained any false illusions about Payne, realizing he would never reform, but it bothered her that he was borrowing money from people who looked up to her and to James Madison. When she sold Montpelier, she had kept a portion of the estate, hoping she could leave it to Payne, thereby giving him a measure of security after she was gone.

Now, she knew, she would have to mortgage that property in order to raise the $6,000. Saying nothing about her intentions to either Richard or Annie, she borrowed $3,000 from the elderly John Jacob Astor, whose fur trading company had made him one of America's wealthiest men. She obtained the other $3,000 from William W. Corcoran, a Washington banker, who granted her the loan because, he wrote, in spite of her troubled finances she was a "strong moral risk."

She sent the money to Payne, the last he would receive from her. Richard Cutts was furious when he learned what she had done, and took even tighter control of her affairs. Dolly regarded the repayment of any debt as a matter of personal honor, and by living frugally she was able to discharge her obligations to Astor and Corcoran in full in the final years of her life.

Dolly was reduced to a state of genteel poverty during the years of the Polk Administration, but her pride was so great that virtually no one knew it. She bought no new clothes, and Annie, who did their marketing, bought the cheapest cuts of meat.

Eventually, however, such friends as Daniel Webster and a future President, Secretary of State James Buchanan, learned of her plight. Thanks to their efforts a bill was introduced simultaneously in both the Senate and House of Representatives in the late autumn of 1847, authorizing the Congress to purchase a trunkload of James Madison's papers from her. There were no serious objections to the bill, and it passed without difficulty. President Polk signed the measure on May 20, 1848, Dolly's eightieth birthday.

Under its terms she would be paid $25,000 for her husband's papers, and Secretary Buchanan was designated as the trustee who would administer the funds. Dolly's need for cash was immediate, and some weeks would pass before she would receive the money, so she decided to raffle off some of her possessions, including several Gilbert Stuart portraits and other works of art that had been displayed at Montpelier.

Buchanan learned of the impending auction, as did Richard Cutts, and they acted swiftly, canceling the affair. Buchanan provided $5,000 of the sum authorized by the government for the purchase of the Madison papers, and this money was used to pay her most pressing obligations. The remaining $20,000 was placed in a trust fund, and Dolly was given the income from the investments the Secretary of State made on her behalf. Her funds were limited, but she enjoyed a measure of security she had not known for many years.

On July 4, 1848, Dolly and Mrs. Hamilton, the former in her eighty-first year and the latter in her ninety-first, were major participants in a special ceremony, the laying of the cornerstone for the Washington Monument in the capital. They rode together in an open carriage, and General Winfield Scott, commander of the Army since 1841, rode at the head of an honor guard of generals and commodores, among them the next President, Major General Zachary Taylor.

Later that day Dolly gave a reception for the more than two hundred guests who had been present at the ceremony. She held her last reception on New Year's Day, 1849, and more than four hundred people stopped in to pay their respects to her. President Polk remarked that "more people went to Mrs. Madison's home than came to our official White House reception."

The last public event she is known to have attended was a gala held at the White House in February, 1849. She wore a gown of black velvet and one of her familiar turbans of white satin, and she looked so regal that Mrs. Polk remarked, "She stands first among our First Ladies."

President Polk took note of the occasion in his diary:

Wednesday, 7th February, 1849.—General notice had been given in the City papers that the President's mansion would be open for the reception of visitors this evening. All the parlours including the East Room were lighted up. The Marine band of musicians occupied the outer Hall. Many hundreds of persons, ladies & gentlemen, attended. It was what would be called in the Society of Washington a very fashionable levee. Foreign Ministers, their families & suites, Judges, members of both Houses of Congress, and many citizens and strangers were of the company present. I stood and shook hands with them for over three hours. Towards the close of the evening I passed through the crowded rooms with the venerable Mrs. Madison on my arm. It was near 12 O'Clock when the company retired.

Although Dolly did not venture out again, she continued to receive visitors at home. The Polks called on her on March 4 soon after Zachary Taylor's inauguration, and later in the day President and Mrs. Taylor stopped in, taking time from their busy schedule to pay their respects to her. The twelfth President was a native of Orange County, Virginia, and had known Dolly since his early childhood. Her record was unique: Married to the fourth

President, she had been well acquainted with the other eleven who held office during her lifetime.

That life drew to a quiet close in the summer of 1849. At eighty-one, Dolly appeared to be withstanding the Washington heat without difficulty, but on July 11 she complained of indigestion. She retired to her bed, and Annie summoned a physician, who told her Dolly was suffering from fatigue. She remained in bed, and at sundown on July 12 she fell into her last deep sleep.

The funeral service was held at St. John's Church on Monday, July 16. President Taylor issued a proclamation making it a day of national mourning. He himself walked at the head of the funeral procession to the church, followed by the Cabinet, the Supreme Court, members of both Houses of the Congress, and the diplomatic corps. There was little room in the church for the general public, but tens of thousands lined Pennsylvania Avenue to watch in silence as the procession passed.

Later that week Dolly Madison was buried beside her husband in the family plot at Montpelier.

Bibliography

Anthony, Katharine, *Dolly Madison: Her Life and Times.* Garden City, N.Y., Doubleday, 1949.

Brant, Irving, *James Madison*, 6 vols. Indianapolis, Bobbs-Merrill, 1941–1961.

Butterfield, Lyman H., et al, eds., *Adams Family Correspondence: December 1761–March 1778*, 2 vols. New York, Atheneum, 1965.

Clark, Allen C., *Life and Letters of Dolly Madison.* Washington, D.C., Press of W. F. Roberts Company, 1914.

Dean, Elizabeth Lippincott, *Dolly Madison, the Nation's Hostess.* Boston, Lothrop, Lee, 1928.

Goodwin, Maud C., *Dolly Madison.* New York, Scribner's, 1909.

Jefferson, Thomas, *Writings*, A. A. Lipscomb and A. E. Bergh, eds., 20 vols. Washington, D.C., Thomas Jefferson Memorial Association of the U.S., 1903–1904.

Ketcham, Ralph, *James Madison: A Biography.* New York, Macmillan, 1971.

Koch, Adrienne, *Jefferson and Madison: the Great Collaboration.* New York, Oxford U. Press, 1964.

Madison, Dolly, *Memoirs and Letters*, Lucia B. Cutts, ed. Boston, Houghton, Mifflin, 1886.

Madison, James, *Letters and Other Writings*, Wm. C.

Rives and Philip R. Fendall, eds., 4 vols. Philadelphia, J.B. Lippincott Co., 1865.

————, *The Papers of James Madison*, Vols. 1–4, Wm. T. Hutchinson et al, eds. Chicago, U. of Chicago Press, 1962–1969.

————, *Writings*, Gaillard Hunt, ed., 9 vols. New York, C. Scribner's Sons, 1900–1910.

Monroe, James, *Papers*, W. C. Ford, ed. Washington, D.C., Government Printing Office, 1904.

Smith, Margaret Bayard, *The First Forty Years of Washington Society*, Gaillard Hunt, ed. New York, 1906.

Index

war with, 158
Bayard, James, 215
Bill of Rights, adoption of, 46
Bonaparte, Elizabeth, 137
Bonaparte, Jerome, 136
Bonaparte, Josephine, fashion influence of, 123
Brionne, André de, 158
Britain. *See* Great Britain.
British, 25. *See also* Great Britain.
  invasion of Chesapeake Bay, 217
  march on Washington, 219
Buchanan, James, 243, 244
Burr, Aaron, 51
  disgrace of, 177
  duel with Hamilton, 156
  in election of 1800, 106, 108
  Madison dislike of, 109
  Madison opinion of, 75
  party alienation of, 110

C

Cabinet
  Jefferson's, 114
  Madison's first, 184
  Madison's second, 210
Calhoun, John C., 206
Capital
  New York as, 47
  Philadelphia as, 48
Carroll, John, 170
Chesapeake Bay, British invasion of, 217
Childlessness of Madisons, 92
City Dancing Assembly, 91
Clay, Henry, 203, 212, 215
Clinton, De Witt, 207
Clinton, George
  as anti-Madison candidate, 180
  death of, 207
  as Jefferson running mate, 156
  and presidential qualifications, 159
Clothing. *See also* Fashion.
  Indian, 174
  plantation, 18
  Quaker, 19, 40
Coles, Betsy, 212
Coles, Edward, 123, 191, 204
Coles, Isaac, 187
Coles, John, visits to, 15
Coles, William, 12
Coles Hill, 13
Collins, Elizabeth, 52, 63
Commerce, problems of American, 179
Confederation, advocates of, 42
Congress
  first meeting of, 47
  purchase of Madison papers by, 240, 244
Constitution
  Madison and planning of the, 43
  ratification of, 46
Constitutional Convention
  calling of, 43
  Madison as delegate to Virginia, 235
Cooking, American style of

(257)

V

W